पुरामंथन
PURĀMANTHANA

पुरामंथन

PURĀMANTHANA

(CURRENT ADVANCES IN INDIAN ARCHAEOLOGY)

Number : 5 **2009**

Editors

A.K. SHARMA

B.R. MANI

C. MARGABANDHU

G.S. KHWAJA

BKP

BHARATIYA KALA PRAKASHAN

DELHI (INDIA)

First Edition : 2009

Published by **C.P. Gautam**
BHARATIYA KALA PRAKASHAN
3421-A, IInd Floor, Narang Colony, Tri Nagar,
Delhi-110035. Telefax : 27393083 Ph. : 32967505 (O)
E-mail: bkp3421@yahoo-co.in
Website : www.bkpbooks.com

ISBN : 978-81-8090-247-5

Laser Type Setting by
A-One Graphics,
New Delhi-1100015

Printed at :
Excel Prints, Naraina, New Delhi.

Cover Front : Row of grainaries and *Snan-kunds* at Sirput
Back : Terracotta Figure

Contents

Editorial

Dear Scholars,

Puramanthana No. 5 is before you. I am sorry for the delay. The anxiety to include as many articles as possible, penned by youngers is one of the reasons. I am happy that the younger genration is slowly picking up.

Presently Archaeology is passing through the decline phase. This happens with every descipline and every aspect of life. Rise and fall and then rise is a natural phenomenon. Let us hope brighter days are ahead. In the intervening period many stalwarts like Shri M.N. Despande, Dr. Mrs. Deb-bala Mitra, Dr. N.R. Banerjee, Shri Jagat Pati Joshi, Dr. S.P. Gupta, Shri M.C. Joshi, Shri K.M. Shrivastava, Dr. W.H. Sidiqqui, Dr. B. Narasimhaiah and Dr. Madhav N. Katti and even younger stars like Dr. L.S. Rao left us awastruck—dificult to fill the gaps. Now the responsibility of you young scholars is much more to raise the flag of our descipline and keep it flying high. That will be the real tribute to the departed stalwarts.

The one stigma put by administrators on us of not writing excavation reports must be wiped out and we have the capability to do so. This will be real tribute to Archaeology. The disturbing tendency to shun field work must be discouraged as archaeology is field work and more field work.

Not paying desired attention to monuments and antiquities and raising only boundry walls is bringing bad name. Research, chemistry, museum and Epigraphy branches are not getting the required attention and incentives. The policy of merging museums with circles has resulted in decline of museum standards.

Hoping for the return of research oriented and hard working days in Archaeology, in Center, States and Research Institutions.

Yours

New Delhi, 22nd Aug., 2009

A.K. Sharma

LIST OF FIGURES

LIST OF PLATES

1

DISCOVERY OF BUDDHA STUPA AT SIRPUR

—A.K. Sharma

Location-Sirpur (Lat. $21^0 25'$ N, Long $82^0 10'$ E) MSL 262 m. now a small village on the right bank of Mahanadi in District Mahasamund of Chhattisgarh. State in India is located east-north-east of Raipur, the present capital of the state.

Presently surrounded by forested area on three sides with a chain of north-south running hills on the east and Mahanadi on the west, the site possesses extensive archaeological remains in an area of nearly 35sq kms. Its northern limit is at Khamtarai on south-east upto Jamnaa-Band at Khirsali, and the Khaaarwa-Band at Achanakpur, both places being 10 kms distance from the Gandheshwar Temple of the present village.

On the basis of so far discovere archaeological and inscriptional evidences Sirpur was the capital of Dakshin-Kosala ruled by Sarabhapurias and Panduvasmi kings from 4th to 10th century A.D. Its ancient name was Sripur as per copper-plate record of Tivara Deva. According to Alexander Cunningham[1], "as it was a great city at that time, it must have been founded some time before."

The present excavation in 2008-09 has now proved this assumption as below the Sarabhapuriya levels structural remains and typical Red Polished Ware with abundance of spouted vessels, shaped out of very fine well levigated clay and well fired, have been found which belong to Satavahana Period i.e from 2nd century BC to 3rd-4th century A.D. (Pl. I) These remains have been unearthed to the north-east of Gandheswar temple and east of an old fort (Beglar-1873-74)[2] or Chota-kila or "Little Fort" surrounded with walls of cut stones (Cunningham[3]), where remains of sprawling township with continuous occupation from 2nd cent. B.C. to 14th century A.D. i.e. from Satavahana period to Sarabhapuriya, Panduvamsi and Kalchuri Periods and later is coming to light. (Pl. II) From the town-ship area, from top levels silver coins of Sultan Alaud-Din Mohammad Shah II (1296-1316 A.D.); of

Khalji Sultans of Delhi, Alaud-Din Khalji (1313-14th A.D.); Mughal Emperors Shahjahan and Aurangzeb (1658-1707 A.D.) and a terracotta seal with Persian legends have been recovered. One of the coins of Aurangzeb bears the mint name as Bandare-e Mubarak Surat.

These finds clearly indicate that Sirpur was a flourishing trade centre even upto the beginning of 18th century A.D., negating the so far believed theory that the town was deserted and turned into ruins after Kalchuris.

Cunningham[1] writes "According to the people, the original name of the place was Savaaripura, because it was here that the female anchoret Savari offered a *Ber* fruit to Ramachandra during his wanderings, which was gratefully aaccepted. In the Ramayana, Savari is represented as a very holy recluse, who lived in the banks of the Pampa River to the west of "Rishyamukha's wood-crowned height". There is no mention of the fruit offering; but this act of Savari is famed all over India, and has been embodied in one of the most popular songs of the people. If, however,Sirpur was the site of Savari's hermitage, then the Mahanadi river must be identified with the Pampaa, and the hills to the east with the Rishikulya mountain. But, as we learn from the Mahabharat that the capital of Chedi was situated on the Suktimati river, and, as we know that the Mahanadi flowed through the country of Chedi, I am more inclined to accept the Mahanadi as the reprehensive of Suktimati as to place the capital of Kosala on its banks.

In *Mahaparinivana Sutta* there is a description that Buddha told his disciple Ananda that on the *samadhi* of Chakravartin kings *Stupa* is erected and such *stupa* should be built on his mortal remains. This *Stupa* should be built at the meeting of four roads.

चातु महापथे रज्जो चक्कवतिस्स यूपं करोति।

Ananda— कथं मयं भन्ते तथागतस्स शरीरे परिपज्जामाति।

Bhddha— अव्यावटा तुम्हे आनन्द होय तथागतस्स सरीर पूजाय।

Ananda— कथंपन भन्ते तथागतस्स सरीरे परिपाज्जितब्ब?

Bhddha— यथा खो आनन्द रज्जो चक्कवतिस्स सरीरे परिपज्जन्ति, एवं तथागतस्य सरीरे पटिपज्जितब्वंति।

Ananda— कथं भन्ते रज्जो चक्कववत्रिस्सम सरीरे पटिपज्जनतीति?

Bhddha— चातुम्महापथे रज्जे चक्कवतिस्स यूप करोन्ति। एवं चातुम्महापथं तथागतस्स यूपो कातब्यो।

This dialogue indicated that Buddha knew about the erection of *stupas* over the *samadhi* of Chakravartins. Construction of *Stupa* over the mortal remains has also been described in *Mahavamsa*. The cult of *Stupa,* which had its origin in a pre-Buddhist cult of the heroized dead, may well have developed within the first decades of the Buddha's death, but it must have received ą great impetus under the patronage of Emperor Asoka. In fact the *Stupa* is the continuation of Vedic funerary cairn or tumulus erected over the mortal remains of distinguished persons. A fine example of mud brick tumulus with *Bhumi-griha* has come to light from Kalibangan, a Harappan site on the banks of ancient Saraswati.[4&5]

Buddha's *parinirvana* took place at Kushinagara in Deoria district of Uttara Pradesha, India which was a capital of Malla kings. After the cremation of Buddha's body Mallas took possession of his mortal remains. Other rulers also wanted share of it. The atmosphere became tense and there appeared possibility of war. Those who wanted share were :

1. Ajatshatru - Rajagriha
2. Shakya - Kapilvastu
3. Buli - Alpakappa
4. Koliya - Ramagrama
5. Malla - Pawa
6. Lichhavi - Vaisali
7. Brahmin - Veetha
8. Malla - Kusinagara

Mallas of Kusinagar wanted the *Stupa* erected at Kusinagar only, the *parinirvana* place of Buddha.

Seeing the war—like situataion, a Brahmin named Drona suggested division of *Dhatu* (mortal remains) into eight parts. This satisfied all and war was averted. Eight *Stupas* were built over these eight parts. This episode has been depicted on the southern and western *Toran-dwars* (gates) of Sanchi Stupa. Along with war scenes eight elephants carrying the relic caskets on their head in a procession has been shown.

When Asoka embraced Buddhism,. in order to popularise stupa-worship, he got removed the ashes from these eight original *Stupas* and erected 84 thousand *stupas* all over his empire.

It will not be out of place to state that Buddha's four main symbols denote four main events of his life :

1. Birth	-	Depiction of white elephant
2. Aquisition of knowledge	-	Bodhi tree
3. Spread of his religion	-	Dharma chakra
4. Parinirvana	-	Stupa

Originally Sanchi *Stupa* was in the form of a mound. At Sanchi the *torana dwaras* were erected in 2nd century B.C. In the beginning Stupas were erected of mud in the form of semicircle *(Anda)* over a platform or *vedi*. As time passed the hemispherical *Anda* started becoming elongated. On top in the centre *Yasti* is erected on which three *Chatras* (circular stones) are put in receding order, biggest at the bottom. *Stupas* are of various sizes. Vaisali *Stupa* is of smaller dimension. Top of platform is used for *pradakshina*. Probably the *Stupa* built by Ashoka had no *harmika* and *chaatra*. At Sanchi over the original *Stupa,* stone coping was done during the Sunga period. During 2nd century B.C. the followers of Hinayana expanded the size of *Stupa*.

During Maurya period in order to keep the sanctity of the *Stupa,* on the ground level it was encircled by creating a *Vedika* at a distance of nearly a meter or so. The space between the *Anda* and this circle was used as *Pradakshina-path* which was used by *Upasakas*. Bharhut, Bodha-Gaya and Amaravati *Vedikas* are examples in this direction.

The Stupa at Sirpur

Hiuen Thsiang, the chinese traveler who visited Kosala (Kiao-SA-LO) in 639 A.D.[6] writes that the capital is about 40 li round. Not far to the south of the city is an old *sanghaarama* by the side of which is a *Stupa* that was built by Asoka-raja. In this place *Tathagata,* of old, calling an assembly, exhibited his supernatural power and subdued the unbelievers. Afterwards Nagarjuna Bodhisattva (Long-meng-pu-sa) dwelt in the *sangharama*. The king of the country was then called Sadvaha (2nd century A.D.). He greatly prized esteemed Nagarjuna and provided him with a city-gate-hut[7]. At this time Ti-po (Deva) Bodhisattva coming from the country of Chi-see-tseu (ceylon), sought to hold a discussion with him. Alexander Cunningham has stated that Sadvaha denoted 'Satvahana'[8].

He also writes that there are about one hundred *sanghaaramas,* and somewhat less than 10,000 priests; they all alike study the teaching of the great Vehicle. There are about seventy Deva temples, frequented by heretics of different persuasions.

Sirpur 2009, Disst. Mahasamund, India

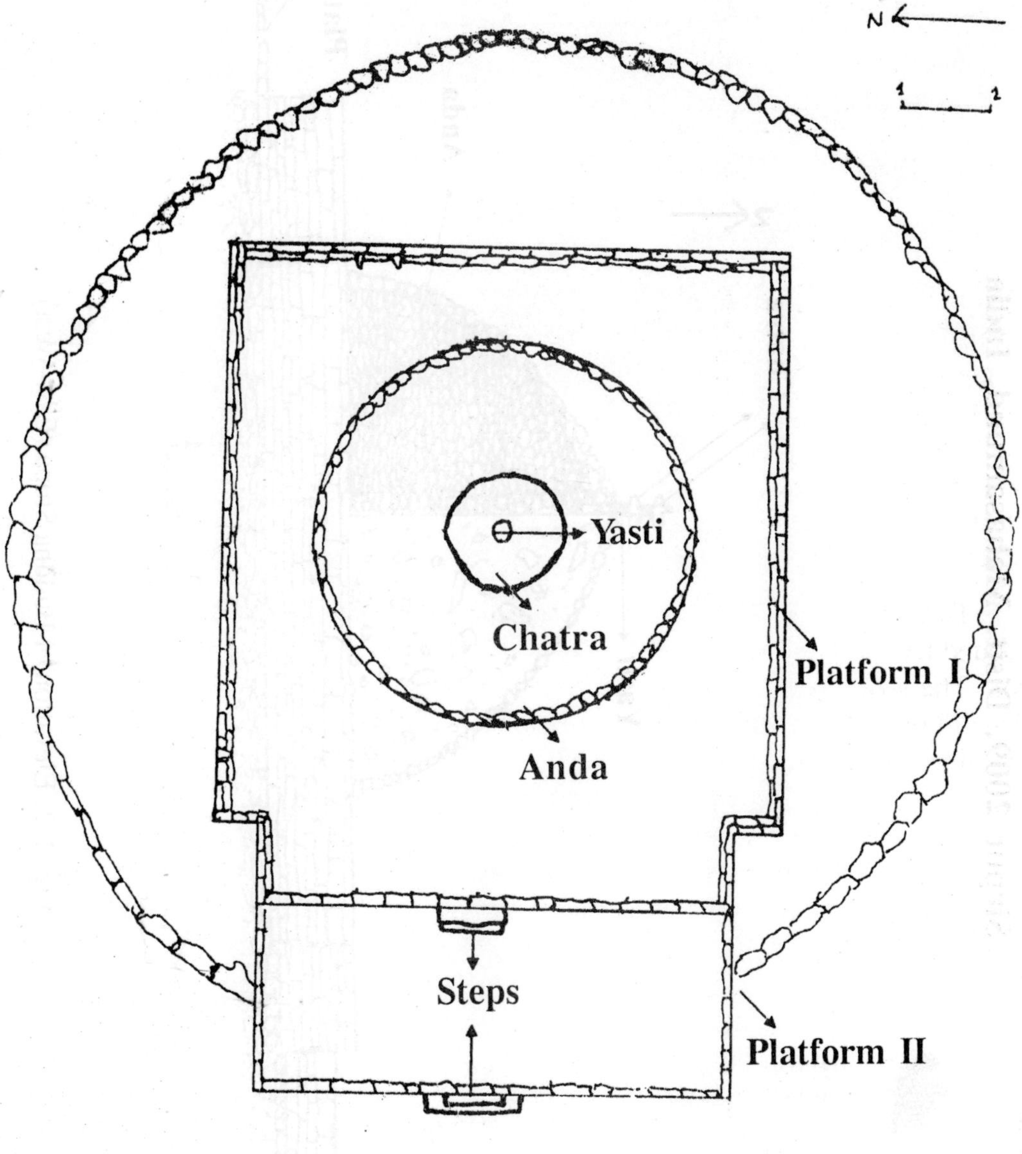

Fig. 1.1. Plan of Buddha Stupa

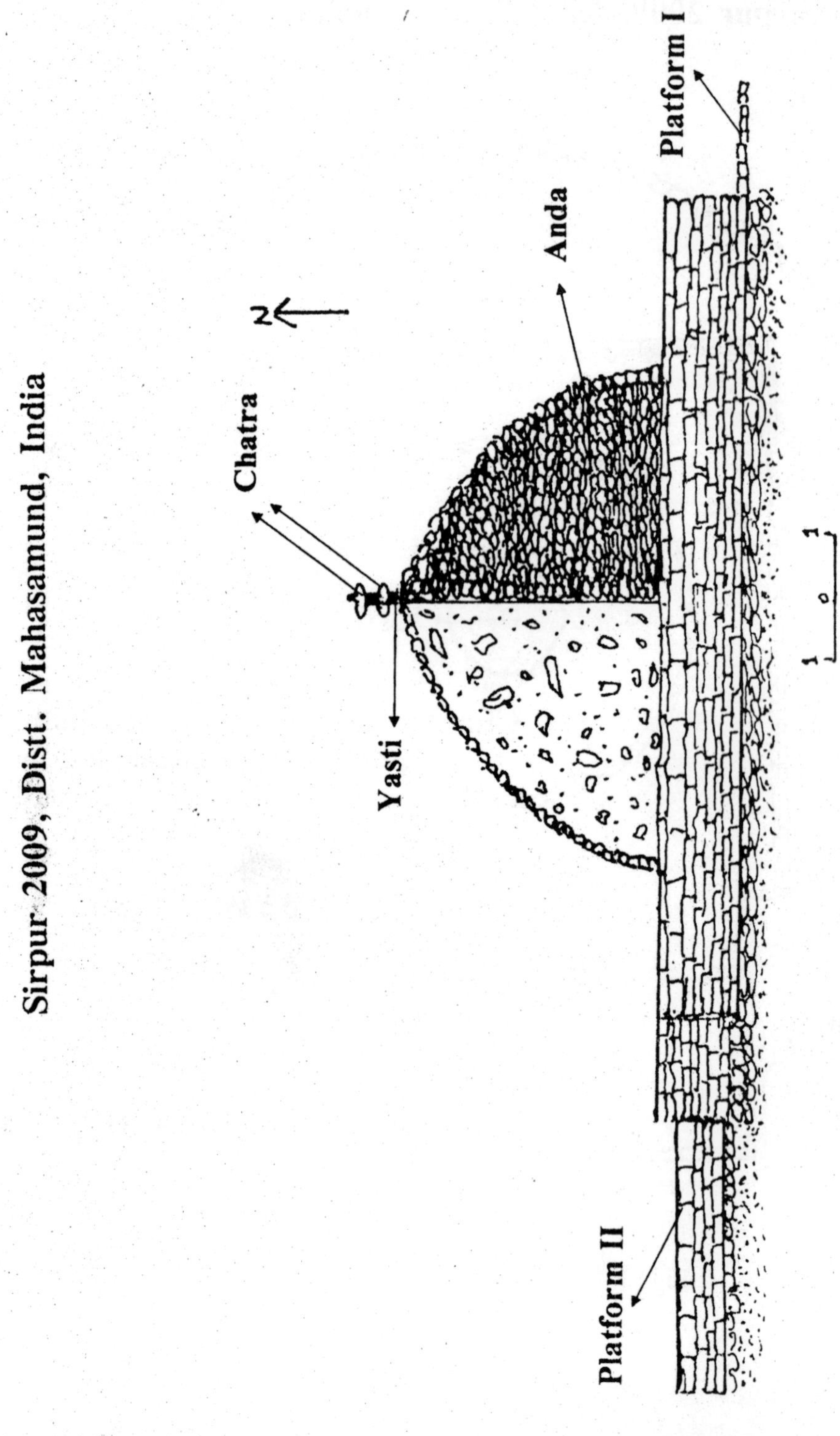

Fig. 1.2. Elevation of Buddha Stupa (East-West)

The soil is rch and fertile, and yields abundant crops. The towns and villages are close together. The population is very dense. The men are tall and of black complexion. The disposition of the people is hard and violent; they are brave and impetuous. There are both heretics and believers here. They are earnest in study and of high intelligence. The king is of the *Kshattriya* race; he greatly honors the laws of Buddha and his virtue and love are far renowned.

According to *Kottahara Sutta*[9], *Buddhaa travelled to Kosala,* an adjoining region of Kalinga to give sermon to the *kottaharakas* or faggot carriers of Kosala. To commemorate the incident, later on, an *arama* was built and named after it, in the region of Kalinga or Kosala.

There is the well-known episode of the *Brahmana* sage Bavari of Kosala, who lived in a place located on the banks of the river Godavari, near Assak region in Dakshinapatha and in the peripheral areas of Mulaka in Andhradesa; and sent his pupils to meet the Buddha and learn from his teachings.[10]

Thus it appears, the Master visited the places beyond Vindhya regions and Buddhism as a religion must have reached the masses even during the life time of the Master.

From the accounts of Megasthanese, it is evident that there existed 30 fortified towns, equipped with elaborate military organization; during 3rd century B.C. in Andhra especially in the regions of Asmaka, Mulaka, Kosala, Vidarbha and Mohisaka. Excavations at Mansar, District Nagpur, Maharastra by the author since 1997-98 has brought to light the military establishment and fortified capital of Satvahana (2nd cent. B.C.-3rd cent. A.D.) named Nandivardhyam proves Megasthanese narration. Therefore it is reasonable to assign the beginnings and early phases of these urban centres to at least a century or a couple of centuries before the visit of Megasthanese[11] i.e. 5th-4th century B.C. Thus it is clear that Kosala had also well established Janapada, like the Janapadas of Noth India. But it is difficult to explain how and why the early Buddhist chronicles failed to mention the very existence of such prominent Janapadas.

The discovery of Stupa south-east of Lakshmana temple and on the north-eastern corner of the ancient Raikera tank solves many puzzles. Recently the author has excavated the remains of a sprawling township to the north of the present village. So far the excavations have yielded four periods of house complexes :

1. Satavahana period - 2nd cent B.C. to 3rd cent A.D.
2. Sarbhapuriya period - 5th -6th cent A.D.

3. Panduvamsi period - 7th to 10th cent. A.D.

4. Kalchuri period - 12th cent. onwards

From the bottom most level, so for excavated, (as the natural soil is yet to be reached) we have recovered typical Red-Polished Ware with profusion of spouted vessssels of different shapes and sizes datable to 2nd -3rd century B.C.-A.D. Taking into account the location of ancient Buddhist monastery (SRP-1) excavated by us in 1999-2000 and the location of ancient city the *Stupa* fits in the description given by Hiuen Thiang. (Pl. II& III)

The original sand stone bulder and mud *Stupa* is spread in an area of nearly 14 x 14 m. The 4.30 m high *Anda* has been raised on a dressed lime stone platform which measures 13.20 x 12.80 m, east-west and north-south respectively. At present the platform consists of eight courses of lime stone rectangular blocks of different sizes and the extant height is 1.20 m. The first course of the dressed stones rest over two courses of boulders which form the base of the platform. These boulders have been kept on well rammed earth mixed with small pebbles and gravel brought from the river. It is learnt that quite a large number of dresed stones were taken away by a rich man from nearby Khamtarai village whose house is built of these dressed stones. This indicates that the platform was still higher. (Pl. IV)

The fourth course from the bottom dressesd course has ribbed concave design on the outer surface.

In the cente of the platform stands a semicircular *Anda* having diameter of 8.80 m. at the base and 2.90 m. at the top. The entire *Anda* is built of sand stone boulders. The boulders vary in size but on an average they are of the size 30 x 20x 8 c.m. From the surface of the platform 26 courses of boulders in very vertical position are visible. Generally the bottom ones are of bigger size, slowly receding in size as we reach the top. The inside of the *Anda* is filled with boulders, pebbles and mud. From the condition of the deposit it is clear that while raising the height of the *Anda*, pebbles, boulders and earth were put layer by layer making them wet and then ramming to make solid mass. On top of *Anda* in the centre stands a stone Chatra. The stone *Yasti* has two grooves at equidistance. Unfortunately at the proximal and the *yasti* is broken. In the two sockets two circular *Chatra* are present. Normally there are three *Chatra's* but as the *Chatra-Yasti* is broken at the lower end the bottom most *Chatra* is missing. The middle *Chatra* is having diameter of 45 cm. while the top one has diameter43 cm. The available height of *Yasti* is 70cm. and girth 45 cm. (Pl. V and VIII)

From the available evidences it is clear that around the platform there was another circle at the ground level having diameter of nearaly 18.0 m. built of huge undressed sand stone boulders. The space between the platform and the circle had baked brick flooring. The size of bricks vary from 40 x 24 x 8 to 38 x 23 x 7 cm. This *Vedica* was created in order to keep the sancity of stupa during Mauryan period. The whole constructional pattern of the original *Stupa* shows that it was built around 3rd cent. B.C. during Asokan period and in this period normally these contained mortal remains of Buddha. As per order's of Asoka these were raised on cross-roads. Sirpur, incidentally, falls on the main trade and religious routes from east-to west i.e. Cuttack to Surat and north-to-south i.e. Varanasi to Kanya Kumari. So it is apparent that Sirpur was a great religious and trade centre right from at least 3rd cent. B.C. to 15th cent. A.D. This has been proved by the discovery of 79 bronze Buddhist images on 13-1-08 and silver coins of Sultanate and Mughal period along with a terracotta seal inscribed with Persian legend.

In later period around 3rd century AD the platform was enlarged on the western side by creating a lower platform measuring 10.50 m. north-south and 6. 10 m. east- west. This is clear from the evidence that in order to create this extra platform the western wall of original platform was demolished and after creating an inset of 0. 60 m. the stones of four coursed platform were inserted inside the main platform. The second construction is of inferior quality as over the base comprising of small pebbles dressed lime stone blocks of different sizes have been laid thus not making even courses. Above the lower most course an inset of 0. 20 m.has been created on all the three sides i.e. north, south and west. The total height is o.70 m. In order to climb this addition two steps in the center of the western wall have been made, while only one step of laterite rectangular dressed stone has beeen made in the centre of the western wall. The solid proof that this addition was done in around 3rd-4th cent. AD is the engraving of compact alphabets reading as ह्ल (hla) (Pl.VII) on one of the two western steps in Gupta-*Brahmi* character of 4th cent. A.D. The second platform was created probably to allow the devotees to have a round of *Anda*. This *Pradakshina path* is 1.85 m. to 4.50 m. (at the corners) wide thus violating the earlier norms. The discovery of this early *Stupa* takes back the date of Sirpur to 5th cent. B.C. and passes through Asokan, Mauryan, Satvahana, Sarabhapuriya to Panduvamsi periods i. e. upto at least 8th century A.D a span of 1300 years. A terracotta model of the above *Stupa* was recovered from one of the Buddha Viharas. The 1.5 cm high *Anda* having diameter of 2.1 cm. is encircled by a circle having 5.5 cm diameter. The model is approximately 300 times smaller than the main structure. (Pl. VIII) The earliest *Stupa* at Pauni, brick built (40 x 30 x 10cms) has diameter of 38.20 meters. The *Pradakshina patha* was about 2.78 meters. It belongs to the Maurya-Sunga period.

The unearthing of nine Buddhist monasteries (two in 1953-56 by Dr. M.G. Dixit and seven by the author from 1999-2000 to 2007-2008); a hoard of 79 bronze Buddhist images in 2008, comprising of Buddha, Bodhisattvas, Jambhala, Buddhist Goddesses, Vajra-model and *Stupa* models clearly show that Buddhism both in Heenayana and Mahayana form was quite popular in the area. The foundations were laid in 3rd century B.C. with the erection of the *Stupa* at Sirpur during Asoka's period.

REFERENCES

1. Alexander Cunningham, *Report of a Tour in the Central Provines and Lower Gangetic Doab* in 181-82, A. S. I., Vol. XVII
2. Beglar, *Report of a tour in the Central Provinces*-1973-74. Archaeological Survey of India, Vol. VII, 108
3. T.W. and C.A.R Rhys Davids (tr.), *Dialogue of the Buddha* (Sacred Books of Buddhists), London, 1910, vol. II, p. 87
4. Sharma, A.K., *The Departed Harappans of Kalibangan,* New Delhi, 1994
5. Sharma, A.K., *Harappan Cemetery at Kalibangan a Demographic Survey,* Puratattava, No. 10, New Delhi, 1978-79
6. *Chinese Accounts of India,* Vol.-4, Translated from the Chinese of Hinen Thsiang by Samual Bead, Calcutta, p. 414
7. *Placed Guards Around His Hut* (Julian)
8. *Ancient Geography of India,* p. 414
9. V. Fausball, The *Jatakas,* The Kottahar-Jakata No. 7, vol. I, pp. 113-116
10. S. Dutta, *Buddhist Mound and Monasteries in India,* 1960, p. 120, and also N. Dutta, *Early monastic Buddhism*, 1941, pp. 193-95 and *Suttanipata*, (Verse 1019)
11. N.S. Ramchandra Murthy, *Excavation at Kotalingala in Karimnagar district of A.P.* (unpublished), article on Kotalingala-an early Historical site in APHC, 1992, pp. 33-34.

2

SIRPUR COPPER-PLATES OF PĀṆḌUVAṀŚI RULERS

—Prabhat Kumar Singh

Introduction

Sirpur, Lat. 21^0 25'N, Long. 82^0 11 'E is a small village on east bank of Mahānadī in district Mahasamund of Chhattisgarh state, India. A hoard of twelve **copper-plates,** were discovered in the course of excavations[1]. They are in four sets of three plates each, called hereafter **Set A, B, C** and **D.** In this paper attempt has been made to decipher and analyse the information contained in them. First set of these four was issued by **Mahā Śivagupta Tivaradeva.** Beside Sirpur, Bonḍā (District-Raigarh) is the other place, from where two sets of copper-plates of both the above ruler were found together on May 5th, 1959.

Salient features

First and last plate of all the sets are inscribed on one side only and middle plates have writings on both sides. Outer surface of the former plates are blank and serve the protection to writings on the opposite side of these plates. The plates of the sets are held together by means of a thick copper ring with shouldered ends, passing through holes cut at the middle, near the margin. Rings are further made to pass through the perforated handle of seals, which are circular in shape and contain three auspicious symbols at top representing religious signs of the granter rulers, two lines of inscription in the cerntre and a full bloom lotus at the bottom. These three zones of depiction on seals are separated by a couple of horizontal lines. Plates are quite smooth and edges have been raised. All plates are in excellent state of preservation. Charters are inscribed width wise. Letters are deeply cut and some of them show through on the other side, especially in case of first and last plates. Following table will enable us to understand :

Sets	A- of Mahāśiva-Tīvaradeva, R.Y.-7	B- of Mahāśiva-gupta, R.Y.-6	C- of Mahāśiva-gupta, R.Y.-11	D- of Mahāśiva-gupta, R.Y.-19
Contents				
Registration Nos.	1136	1137	1138	1139
Size (WxHxT)	22.5x13.5x0.3 cm	21.5x13.5x0.3 cm	20.5x12.5x0.3 cm	20.0x12.5x0.4 cm
Rings (Dia.xThick-ness)	12.7x1.2 cm	12.7x0.9 cm	11.6x1.0 cm	11.5x1.2 cm
Mudrās (Dia.x Thickness)	8.5x2.0 cm	9.0x2.0 cm	9.5x1.5 cm	9.5x2.0 cm
Figrues on Mudrā				
Upper	*Cakra-Garuḍa-*	*Triśula-Nandi-*	*Triśula-Nandi-*	*Triśula-Nandi-*
(Right-Middle-Left)	*Śankha*	*Kamanḍalu*	*Kamanḍalu*	*Kamanḍalu*
Centre	Legend	Legend	Legend	Legend
Lower	*Padma*	*Padma*	*Padma*	*Padma*
Lines	10+10+9+10 =39	7+7+7+6 =27	7+7+7+7 =28	7+7+7+7 =28
Letter's size (Average)	0.75 cm	1.4 cm	1.2 cm	1.2 cm

The ***lipi*** is **box-headed** variety of Central Indian alphabets. On the basis of palaeography, charter of **Tīvaradeva** could be placed in second half of seventh century A.D. and those of **Mahāśivagupta** in first half of eighth century A.D. **Language** is **sanskrit,** in a mixture of prose and verse. Except legend on ***mudrā*** and six imprecatory and benedictory stanzas at the end of these records, the inscriptions are in verse throughout. All inscriptions are dated in regnal year of donor kings. These inscriptions have been edited here for the first time from original specimens.

SIRPUR PLATES (SET-A) OF MAHĀŚIVA TĪVARADEVA: R.Y.-7[2]

This is first charter of **Tīvaradeva,** discovered at Sirpur in particular and fourth in general, so far. Its drafting, resembles in many ways to his earlier grants of viz., **Bondā**[3], **Rājim**[4], and **Balodā**[5] plates. Inscription begins with auspicious word

'Om', articulated symbolically. Then it contains a canto in honour of reigning king **Tīvaradeva,** who is described as an ornament of three worlds, a fortunate pillar supporting stately home that is family of kings and chief of all performers of meritorious activities. It is followed by the name of **Śrīpura,** whence the donation was issued. It would not be out of place to mention here that his all other grants ware also issued from the same place i.e., his capital. A long prose passage in introductory portion of the grant, describes about **Mahāśiva Tivaradeva,** son of **Nannadeva** of the **Pāṇḍuvaṁśa** and grand son of **Indrabala,** in a hyperbolic way. He is said to have obtained lordship, over entire **Kosala,** and meditated upon the feet of his parents and to have been a dedicated worshipper of god Viṣṇu, as he is called here *paramavaiṣṇava*. It is said that a number of chiefs who had acquired the five ***mahāśabadas***[6] had ends of their crown rubbed at his feet.

He informs the residents of village **Pañcakuṭya,** sited in *bhoga* of **Anangapalla,** that he had donated this village, for increase of spiritual merit of his parents and of his own self, to Brāhmaṇa **Maṣidevopādhyāya,** who belongs to **Bhārdvāja** *gotra* and ordered them to give *bhāga* (royal share of produce) and *bhoga* (periodical offerings) to the grantee regularly. The grant was intended to last for ever, approved with it right to the *nidhi* (hidden treasure), *upanidhi* (minor underground deposits), all taxes and release from the entry of *cāṭas* (irregular soldiers) and *bhaṭas* (regular soldiers).

Future kings are exhorted to preserve the grant and six imprecatory stanzas, four of them in the name of Vyāsa, telling advantage accruing from making and maintaining land-grants and sufferings resulting from their disobedience are quoted in support of this exhortation.

Grant was issued on **twenty eighth day of the month of *Pauṣa*[7] in seventh regnal year of the king.** Here year and day of month are inscribed only in figures. It doesn't record the name of engraver[8]. The legend on ***mudrā*** meanings- 'The charter of illustrious **Tīvaradeva,** who is overlord of this Kosala, endures as long as the existence of moon and stars, for increase of religion.''

As for localities mentioned in present grant, **Śrīpura** is well identified with present day Sirpur, capital town of Pāṇḍuvaṁśīns. **Anangapalla** *bhoga* could be identified with **Anarghavallī** *viṣaya* mentioned in Śivarīnārāyaṇa copper-plate[9] of Kalachuri king Ratnadeva II. Mirashi[10] is of the opinion that this place was situated in the area of modern Janjgir district. **Pañcakuṭya,** the donated village, cannot now be traced.

TEXT[11]

First Plate (Plate-I)

०१. ओम्[१२] (।*) जयति जगत्त्रय तिलक: क्षितिभृत्कुलभवन मङ्गलस्तम्भ: (।*) **श्रीमत्तीव**-

०२. **रदेवो** धौरेय: सकल पुण्यकृताम् (।। १ ।।*) स्वस्ति **श्रीपुरा**त्समधिगत पञ्चम-

०३. हाशब्दानेकनत नृपतिकिरीटकोटिकोटिघळ्ट चरणनखदर्प्प (र्प) णोद्भासितो-

०४. पकण्ठदिङ्मुख: प्रकट रिपुराजलक्ष्मि: (क्ष्मी:) केशपाशाकर्ष्ष (र्ष) णदुर्ल्ल (र्ल) लितपाणि-

०५. पल्लव: निशितनिस्तृङ्श[१३] घनघातपातितारिद्विरदकुम्भमण्डलग-

०६. लद्बहलशोणित सदासिक्तमुक्ताफलप्रकरमण्डितरणाङ्गण-

०७. विविधरत्नसंभारलाभलोभ (प) विजृम्भमाणारिक्षारवारिवाडवानलश्चन्द्रोद-

०८. य इवकृतकरोदेग१४ क्षीरोद इवाविर्भूतोनेकातिशायिरत्न सम्प१५ । गरूत्मा-

०९. निव भुजङ्गोद्धार चतुर (:) परामृष्टशत्रुकलत्रनेत्राञ्जनकोमलकपोल-

१०. कुङ्मुमपत्रभङ्ग: शिष्टाचारव्यवस्था परिपालनैकदत्तचित्त: (।*) अपि च(।*)

Second Plate : Obverse Side (Plate-II)

११. प्रक्तने[१६] तपसि यशसि रहसि चेतसि चक्षुषि वपुषि च पूजितो जनेन (ना)-

१२. क्लिष्टतया नितान्तमवितृप्तो गूडोगाड[१७] स्वच्छ: प्रसन्नो यौवनेन चाप्लङ्कृ-

१३. त: स्वमि[१८] भवन (न्न) प्यबहुलपनोनज्झित कुतृष्टोपि[१९] नितान्तत्यागि (गी) रिपुजन-

१४. प्रचण्डोपि सो (सौ) म्यदर्शनो भूतिविभूषणोप्यपरूष स्वभाव: किञ्चासन्तु-

१५. ष्टो धर्म्मर्जनेन[२०] सप्प (म्प) ल्लाभे स्वल्प: क्रोधेन प्रभावे लुब्धोयशसि न

१६. परवित्तापहारे स (श) क्त: सुभाषितेषु न कामिनी क्रीडासु प्रतापने-

१७. लक्कधाशेष रिपुकुलतूलराशिस्तुहिन शिशैलधवलयशोरशिप्रका-

१८. शितदिगन्त: कान्त: प्रकृत्या **श्रीमदिन्द्रव (ब) ल** सूनोरलङ्कृत **पाण्डुवङ्शस्य श्रीनत्र**-

१९. **देवस्य** तनय: प्र(प्रा) प्त सकल कोसलाधिपत्य: स्वपुण्य सम्भार प्रशमित शे-

२०. ष जगदुप्रद्रव: स्वप्रज्ञासूचीसमुदृ (द्धृ) ताखिलकण्टक: **परमवैष्णवो**

Second Plate : Reverse Side (Plate-III)

२१. मातापित्रि (तृ) पादानुध्यात (:*) **श्रीमहाशिवति (ती) वरराज:** कुशली (।।*) **अनङ्गपल्लभोगि (गी) य**-

२२. **पत्र्चकुट्याम्**प्रतिवासिन: सम (मा) ज्ञापयति।। विदितमस्तु भवता:

२३. यथास्माभिरय ग्रामायावद्रविशशितारकिरण प्रतिहतघ (घो) र (रा) न्धः;

२४. कारं जगदवतिष्ठते तावदुपभोग्य: सनिधि (:*) सोपनिधिरचाटभट-

२५. प्रा (प्र) वेश्य: सर्वकरसमेतो **भारद्वाजसगोत्राय मषिदेवोपा**-

२६. **क्ध्या:** यायर१ मातापित्रोरात्मनश्च पुन्या (ण्या) भिवृद्धये टदयनद्य

२७. प्रतिपादित इत्यपलभ्य[२२] यथोचितं भोगभागमुपनयन्त:[२३] सु-

२८. खंप्प्रतिवत्स्यथेति[२४]।। भाविनश्च भूमिपालानुद्दिश्येदमभिधीयते (।*) भूमि-

२९. प्रदादिवि ललन्त[२५] पतन्हि हन्त हृत्वा महीं नृपतयो नरके नृश (शं) ङ्शा (सा:) (।*)

Third Plate (Plate-IV)

३०. एतद्वायं[२६] पर (रि) कलरूय चलाञ्च लक्ष्मी मायुस्तथा कुरूत यद्भवतामभीष्टम्(।। २ ।।*)

३१. अपि च (।*) रक्षापालनयोस्तावत्फलं सुगतिदुर्गती (।*) को नाम स्वर्ग-

३२. मुत्सृज्य नरके प्रतिपद्यते (।। ३ ।।*) व्यास गीताश्चात्रश्लोकानुदाहरन्ति अ-

३३. ग्नेर पत्यं प्रथमं सुवर्ण्ण भूव्वै (वैं) ष्णवी सूरूर्यासुताश्च गाव: (।*) दत्तास्त्र-

३४. यस्तेन भवन्ति लोकायम्काञ्चनं गाञ्च महीञ्चदघा (द्या) त् (।। ४ ।।*)

३५. षष्टि वर्ष सहस्त्राणि स्वग्गे (र्गे) मोदति भूमिद: (।*) आच्छे (क्षे) प्ताच्चानुमन्ता

३६. च्चातोन्येव नरके वसेत् (।। ५ ।।*) बहुभिर्व्वसुधा दत्ताराजभि: (:) सगरादिभि: (।*)

३७. यस्य यस्य यदा भूमिस्तस्य तस्यतदाफलं (।। ६ ।।) स्वदत्तां परदत्तम्वा यत्नाद्र-

३८. क्ष युधिष्ठिर (।*) महिमहिमता [२७] श्रेष्ठदानाश्रेयोनुपालनमिति (।। ७ ।।*) **स**[२८] **७ पौष**-

३९. **दिन २८** (।*)

Mudrā (Plate -V)

०१. श्रीमत्ति (त्ती) वरदेवस्य कोसलाधिपतेरिदं (क्रम) (।*)

०२. शासनं धर्मवृद्धयर्त्थ स्थिरमाचन्द्रतारकं (कम्) (।। ८ ।।*)

SIRPUR PLATES (SET-B) OF MAHĀŚIVAGUPTA: R. Y. -6

Sixteen copper-plates of **Mahāsivagupta** have already been discovered from **Bāradulā**[29], **Bonḍā**[30], **Lodhiyā**[31], **Malhāra**[32], and **Sirpur**[33]. Counting current three grants, Sirpur itself exposed a dozen of copper- plates. It is remarkable that Sirpur is the place, whence, copper-plates of Mahāśivagupta, occurred in hoards, so far. His nine charters were found here by accident in surrounding area of Bāleśvara Bhaṭṭāraka temple group (SRP-6-9) in April 1978 just near the eastern side of Mahāśivagupta's residence. Present nine plates are earlier amongst his all dated charters discovered so far, and were issued in the period of first two decades of king's reign. These plates are much akin, especially in drafting manner, to his prior reported grants. Traditionally, existing record starts with ***Om,*** inscribed symbolically as usual. Then it contains a prose passage in praise of **Mahāśivagupta** and narrates about him—'He is dedicated to the feet of his father and mother, prime of the Māheśvaras[34], born in Somavamśa and is son of illustrious ***Harṣadeva,*** like Kārttikeya is of Kṛtivasas[35]—is in good health, has acquired all merits of conqueror through perfection of admirable discipline, effected in particular by implementing all the 'political sciences' he is a harbour for virtuous and his great success has been brought about by his superior valour, brains and potency." **Object** is to record the village-grant given by him. After having paid respect to Brāhmaṇas in village **Pillāsunya,** situated in ***Devabhoga,*** he issues command, by means of this copper-plate charter, to householders being inhabitants of that village, that he had given away this village, after an offering of kwater, for the increase of religious merit of his parents and ownself, to the Brāhmaṇa **Bāḍābhaṭṭa,** inhabitant of **Lāṭa** *viṣaya,* who belongs to **Bhārdvāja** ***gotra*** of **Vājasaneya** ***śākhā*** (of the ***Yajueveda)*** on the occasion of Solar-eclipse, ***amāvasyā tithi*** of the month of **Āṣāḍha**[36], and ordered them to give *bhāga* and *bhoga* to donee regularly. The grant, which was approved with it right to the *nidhi, upanidhi,* all taxes and release from the entry of *cāṭas* and *bhaṭas.* The same 'exhortation' to future kings is given here as in above record. It was issued in **sixth year** of the increasingly victorious reign of **Mahāśivagupta,** on **sixteenth day**[37] of the month of **Āṣāḍha.** Here regnal year is incised both in words and figures while day of the month, only in figure. Kṛiṣṇā, son of Stambha, was scriber of the present record. Legend on ***mudrā*** meanings—'The charter of illustrious Śivagupta, son of king Harṣagupta, who is possessed of good qualities, endures as long as survival of the world.'

The localities mentioned in present grant, ***Devabhoga*** may be present *tehsil* headquarter of same name in Dhamatari district. Nowadays, this place is well known for its alexandrite (diamond) wealth. It has occured in some previous records with least variations. Sirpur plate (No. 6) of Mahāśivagupta (R.Y.-46)[38] and Kaṭaka plates[39] of Mahābhavagupta Bhīmaratha referred it as *Devībhoga* while Terāsinghā plates of Parvatadvāraka Mahārāja Tuṣṭikara as Debhogaka.[40] **Lāṭa** *visaya* generally signifies Central and Southern Gujarat, between Māhī and Tāpī[41] but in some other records, it is said to have included the territory of north of Māhī as far as Kairā[42] The granted village **Pillāsunya,** cannot now be traced.

TEXT[43]

First Plate (Plate-VI)

०१. ओम्[४४] (।*) स्वस्त्यशेषक्षिति (ती) श (ष) विद्यापभ्यास विशेषासदित महनी-

०२. य विनयसपत्स (सम्) पादित सकल विजिगीषु गुणोगुण व-

०३. त्समाश्रय प्रकृष्टतर शौर्य्य प्रज्ञा प्रभाव संभावित महाभ्यु-

०४. दय (:) कार्त्तिकेय इव कृत्तिवाससो राज्ञ (:) श्री हर्षदेवस्य सु-

०५. नु:[४५] सोमवङ्शसंभव: परममाहेश्वरो मातापितृपादानुध्यात

०६. **श्री महाशिवगुप्तराज** कुशली ।। **देवभोगीय पिल्लासुन्य** ग्रा-

०७. म ताम्रशासनेन ब्राह्मणां संपु (पु) ज्य प्रतिवासिन: समाज्ञाप-

Second Plate : Obverse side (Plate-VII)

०८. यति (।*) विदितमस्तु भवतों यथास्माभिरयं ग्राम: सनिधी: (धि:) सोपनिधी (धि:)

०९. आचाटभट प्रवेश सर्व्व करादान समेतो मातापित्त्रोरात्मनश्च

१०. पुण्यभिबृ (वृ) द्धये **लाट विषय वास्तव्य वाजसनेय भारद्वाजस-**

११. **गोत्त्रा (त्रा) य बाडाभट्टा** यौदकपूर्व्वा **अ (आ) षाढामावास्यां सूर्य्योपरा-**

१२. **गे** प्रतिपादित इत्यवगम्य भवद्भि: समुचितं भोगभागमुपन-

१३. यद्भि: सुखंप्रतिवस्तब्य (व्य) मिति ।। भाविनश्च भूमिपालानुदिष्ये द-

१४. मभिधि (धी) यते भूमि प्रदादिवि ललन्ति पतन्ति हन्त हृत्वा मही नृ-

Second Plate : Reverse side (Plate-VIII)

१५. पतयो नरके नृशङ्त् (नृशंसा:) एतद्व (द्ब) यंपरिकलय्य चलाञ्च लक्ष्मी मा-

१६. युस्तथा कुरूत यद्भवतामभीष्ट (टं) (।। १ ।।*) अपि च (।*) रक्षापालनयोस्तावत्फ-

१७. ल (लं) सुगति दुर्ग्गती कोनाम स्वर्गमुच्छ्रित्य नरकं प्रतिपद्यते (।। २ ।।*) व्या-

१८. स गीता (तां) ष्चात्त्र श्लोकानुदाहरन्ति (।*) अग्हनेरपत्यं प्रथमं सु-

१९. वर्ण [४६] भूर्व्वैष्णवी सूर्य्यसुताश्च गावः दत्तात्त्रयस्तेन भवन्ति लोका-

२०. यः[४७] काञ्चनं गाञ्च महीञ्च दद्यात् (।। ३ ।।*) षष्टिवर्षसहस्त्राणि स्वर्ग्गे

२१. मोदति भूदः[४८] आक्षेप्ता चानुमन्ता च त्ता (ता) न्येव नरके वसेत् (।। ४ ।।*)

Third Plate (Plate-IX)

२२. बहुभि[४९] र्वसुधा दत्ता राजभिः सगरादिभिः यस्य यस्य

२३. यदा भूमि तस्य तस्य तदा फलं (।। ५ ।।*) स्वदत्तां परदत्ताम्बा (वा) यत्ना-

२४. द्रक्ष युधिष्ठिरः[५०] महीं मही (हि) मतां श्रेष्ठ दानाश्रेयोनुपा-

२५. लनमिति (।। ६ ।*) प्रवर्द्धमान विजयराज्ये सम्ब (व) त्सरे **ष**-

२६. **ष्ठे ६ । आषाढ दिवसु १० ५ १** आविः प्रकुर्व्वताशिल्यं (पं) पुण्यं

२७. चाक्षयमित्सता **स्तम्भाय्य** सूनुनोत्कीर्ण **कृष्णाय्यनैव** शासनं ।।

Mudrā (Plate-X)

०१. राज्ञ (:) श्री हर्षगुप्तस्य सूनो (:) सद्गुणशालिन (:)

०२. शासनं शिवगुप्तस्य स्थितमाभुवनस्थिते (:) (।।*)

SIRPUR PLATES (SET-C) OF MAHĀŚIVAGUPTA: R.Y.-11

Introductory portion of present inscription is same as above. After having paid respect to Brāhmans in village **Aḍakeraka,** belonging to **Svalpśarkarāmārga,** the king **Mahāśivagupa,** issued instructions to all royal officers, headed by *Samāhartṛ* (collector) and the *Samnidhātṛ* (royal treasurer), to those who are temporarily posted there, along with traders and inhabitants of that village, that he had donated this village, for increase of religious merit of his parents and of his own self, to Brāhmaṇa **Bhaṭṭa Nandikumāra** of **Kāmakāyana** *gotra* of **Vahavṛca** *Śākhā.*

Descriptions of rights that come with grant is mostly same as previous record only adding here with immunity from all impositions and impose fines for the ten offences. Grant is dated only in words. It was issued on **fifth day of bright fortnight of the month Jyeṣṭha, in eleventh regnal year** of increasingly victorious reign, evidenyly of Mahāśivagupta. It was incised by **Golāyya,** son of *akṣaśālika* (goldsmith) **Boppanāga.** He (Boppanāga) who was son of *akṣaśālika* **Gotranāga,** had also inscribed Bondā and Balodā plates of **Tīvaradeva**[51]. Son of **Golāyya,** incisor of present record, **Nāgadeva,** engraved first (R.Y.-52) and seventh (R.Y.-48) sets of Sirpur copperplates, belonging to the earlier hoard of Mahāśivagupta.[52]

Now, on the basis of available evidences, genealogy of *akṣaśālika* **Golāyya** can be draw as :

Gotranāga
↓
Boppanāga
↓
Golāyya
↓
Nāgadeva

Legend on seal is same as Set-B.

As for the places mentioned in present charter, **Svalpśarkarāmārga** is already known from two earlier Sirpur copper-plates[53] of Mahāśivagupta. Svalpa prefix in above place name indicates that there were two places named Śarkarā, one was small and second was big. Fortunately forthcoming plates mention the name of **Bṛhaccharkarāmārga,** on which we will discuss later. Suffix *mārga* denotes that both were subdivisions of Pāṇḍuvamśīns territory. It seems that before turning as subdivision headquarter it was a village. Pīparadulā plates[54] of Śarabhapurīya king Narendera mentions the name of village Śarkarāpadra located in Nandapura *bhoga.* It has been identified with Sānkarā situated in Sarangarh *tehsil* of Raigarh district. Since grantee of Sirpur plates[55] was hailed from Nandapura so equation of **Svalpśarka-rāmārga** with Śarkarāpadra and both with modern Sānkarā appears appropriate.

TEXT[56]

First Plate (Plate-XI)

०१. ओम्[५७] (।*) सवस्त्यशेषक्षितीश (ष) विद्याभ्यास विशेषासादित महनि (नी) य विनय

०२. सम्पत्सम्पादित सकल विजिगि (गी) षु गुणोगुणवत्समाश्रय प्रकृ-

०३. ष्टतर शौर्य्य प्रज्ञा प्रभाव सवम्भावित महाभ्युदय (:) कार्त्तकेय[५८] इ-

०४. व कृत्तिवाससो राज्ञ (:) **श्री हर्षदेवस्य** सुनू[५९] **सोमवङ्श** स-

०५. म्भवः परममाहेश्वरो मातापितृपादानुध्यातः[६०] **श्री महाशिवगु**-

०६. **प्त** राजः कुशलि (ली)।। **स्वल्प शर्करामार्गीय अडकेरके** ब्राह्मणा (णां) संम्पू-

०७. ज्य यथा काहलाध्यासिब्यवहारिणः सकरणाननोनपिसमाह

Second Plate : Obverse side (Plate-XII)

०८. तृ सन्निधातृ प्रभृतिः ।[६१] सर्व्वराजपुरूषा (न्) प्रतिवासिनश्च सनि-

०९. दिशति[६२] (*) विदितमस्तु भवतां यथा स्माभिरय (यं) ग्रामः सनिधीः (धि) सोप-

१०. निकधरचाटभट प्रवेशः सर्व्वकरादान सहितः सदशापराधः

११. सद्वोपद्रव[६३] विवर्जिजतः मातापित्रोरात्मनश्च पुण्याभिवृद्ध-

१२. ये **कामकायन सगोत्राय** वह्वच **भट्ट नन्दिकुमारय** उटक-

१३. पूर्व्वकर्माचन्द्रार्क समकालोपभेगार्थ ताम्रशासनेन प्रतिपादि-

१४. त इत्यवगम्यास्य समुचित (तं) भोगभाग मुपनयद्भिः भव-

Second plate : Reverse side (Plate-XIII)

१५. द्भी सुखंप्रतिवस्तब्य (व्य) मिति ।। भाविनश्च भूमिपालानुद्दश्ये

१६. दमभिधि (धी) यते भूमि प्रदादिवि ललन्ति पतन्ति हन्ति हृत्वा

१७. मही नृपतयो नरके नृशसा (शंसाः) एतद्व (द्ध) यं परिकलरूय चला-

१८. ञ्च लक्ष्मि (क्ष्मी) मायुस्तथा कुरूत यद्भवतामभीष्टं (।। १ ।।*) अपि च (।*)

१९. रक्षा पालनयोस्तावत्फलं सुगति दुर्गति (ती) कोनाम स्वर्ग्ग

२०. मुत्स्रिज्[६४] नरकंप्रतिपक्कयते (।। २ ।।*) ब्या (व्या) सगीतांशचात्रश्लोकानुदाह-

२१. रन्ति (।*) अग्नेरपत्यं प्रथमं सुवर्ण भूर्वेष्णवि[६५] सूर्य्यसुता

Third plate (Plate-XIV)

२२. श्च गाव (:) दत्तात्रयस्तेन भवन्ति लोकाय काञ्चन (नं) गाञ्चमहीञ्चु[६६] दद्या[६७] (।। ३ ।।*)

२३. षषिट वर्ष सहस्त्र (स्त्रा) णि स्वर्ग्गे मोदति भूमिदः आच्छेत्ता[६८] चानुमन्ता च-

२४. ताण्ये (न्ये) व नरके वसेत् (।। ४ ।।*) बहुभिर्व्वसुधा दत्ता राजभि सगरादिभिः

२५. यस्य यस्य यदा भूमि तस्य तस्य तदा पलं (।। ५ ।।*) स्वदतां पर-

२६. दताम्वायत्नाद्रक्ष युधिष्ठिर (महीं*) महीमतां श्रेष्ठ दानाश्रेयोनु-

२७. पालनमिति ।। प्रवर्द्धमान विजयराज्ये सम्ब (म्व) त्सरे एकादशमे ज्येष्ठ-

२८. शुक्लपक्ष पञ्चमां उत्कि (की) र्ण आका (अक्ष) शालिक बोप्पनाग नुनना गोलाय्यन

Mudra

०१. राज्ञः श्री हर्षगुप्तस्य सूनोः सद्गुणशालिनः।

०२. शासनं शिवगुप्तस्य स्थितमाभुवन स्थिते ।।

SIRPUR PLATES (SET-D) OF MAHĀŚIVAGUPTA: R.Y.-19

Beginning with ***Om*** symbol, inscription set up the genealogy and personality of **Mahāśivagupta,** very identical to above both charters. After having paid respect to Brāhmaṇas in village **Vaidya Palāśapadraka,** situated in **Bṛhaccharkarāmārga,** the king **Mahāśivagupta,** issued command by this charter, to all chief royal officers, dedicated to his service, headed by *Samāhatṛ and Samnidhātṛ,* who used to come there from time to time and meet the householders being inhabitants of that village with their headman, that he had donated this village, for the increase of religious merit of his parents and of his own self, to Brāhmaṇa **Bhaṭṭa Bhavadeva** and **(Bhaṭṭa) Janārdana,** both are real-brothers and inhabitants of plains of **Śrīpura,** belong to **Bhāradvāja** *gotra* of **Taittiriya** *śākhā* (of the *Krṣṇa Yajurveda)* on request of **Śrī Bhavaguptarājadeva,** at occasion of **lunar eclipse,** *purṁima tithi* of the month of ***Caitra.***

The rights that come with grant are same as previous record. It was issued in **nineteenth regnal year** of increasingly victorious reign of illustrious Mahāśiva-guptarājadeva, on **thirteenth day** of the month. Name of the incisor is unknown from this grant, due to omission or oversight.

As for localities and personalities are concerned, **Bṛhaccharkarāmārga** can be identified with Śarkarālaka mentioned in Sirpur stone inscription[69] of *ācārya* Buddhaghoṣa. Jain recognized Śarkarālaka to Guḍaśarkaraka mentioned in Senkapāṭa stone inscription of Mahāśivagupta and make it equal to modern Sānkarā.[70] His consideration abour its location, 13 mile in west direction of Sirpur, is not exact. It is situated on right bank of river jonka, 30 mile north-east of Sirpur. **Vaidya Palāśapadraka,** the donated village, may be Pārāsivanī, sited on the bank of same river. The area being on the bank of river Jonka is full fo **Palāśa (*Buta frondose*)** trees, locally known as Parasā.[71] From **Palāśa,** the river name Palāśinī originates, which is identified with Jonka. It is a tributary of Mahānadī and Sānkarā connects its plains.[72] **Śrīpura,** is already recognized with present day Sirpur. **Śrī Bhavagupta-rājadeva,** on whose request present grant was issued, is a new personality found in charters of MahāŚivagupta, so far. We have seen that Mahāśivagupta released land-grants on request of his maternal uncle **Bhāskaravarmā**[73], wives **Ammādevī,**[74] **Abbanibbaddi.**[75] He also issued copper plates for **Amaradevī**[6] and **Śivanandina**[77] who appear to be royal family members. So, **Bhavaguptarājadeva** was definitely one of the members of **Pāṇḍuvamśa,** (early- Somavamśa) and most probably he was prince, as he is adorned here with title of **rājadeva** and is not other than Mahābhavagupta I, popularly known as Janmejaya-I, of Somavamśa, who ruled from Orissa. All inscriptions[78] of Mahābhavagupta I, mention Mahāśivagupta with high respect and honour. Sastri[79] also accepts - 'There are definite indications that they were intimately connected with, and probably belong to Pāṇḍuvamśa.''

Thus, now there should be no doubt in relationship between Pāṇḍuvamsīns and Somavamśīns. The latter was a branch of former who migrated to easts of Sirpur, in search of a new and safe capital because eyes of Tripurī Kalachuris were syayed on their western boundaries.

TEXT[80]

First plate (Plate-XV)

०१. ओम्[८१] (।*) स्वस्तयशेषक्षिति (ती) ष विद्याभ्यास विशेषासादित महनि (नी) य विन-

०२. य संम्पत्सपादित[८२] सकल विजिगि (गी) षु गुणोगुणवत्समाश्रय प्रकृ-

०३. ष्टतर शौर्य्य प्रज्ञा प्रभाव सम्भावित महाभ्युदय (:) कार्त्तिकेय

०४. इव कृतिवाससो राज्ञः **श्री हर्षदेवस्य** सूनू[८३] **सोमवङ्श** स-

०५. म्भव (:) परम माहेश्वरो मातापितृपादानुध्यात **श्री महाशिवगुप्त**

०६. **राज** कुशली । **बुहच्छक्कर्रामागर्गाय वैद्य पलाशपद्रके** । ब्राह्मणा सं-

०७. पुज्य (पूज्य) सप्रधानात्प्रतिवासिनो यथाकालाध्यासिनस्समाहर्त्तृ सन्निधा-

Second Plate : Obverse side (Plate-XVI)

०८. तृ प्रकुखानन्याङश्चास्मत्पादोपजीविनस्सर्व्वराज पुरूषा समाज्ञाप-

०९. यति । विदितमस्तु भवतां यथास्मभिरयं ग्राम (:) सानिधिः[८४] सोपनिधिस्सद-

१०. शापराधस्सर्वकरादान समेतः सर्व्वपि (पी) डा वर्ज्जितः प्रतिषिद्धच्चाटभट

११. प्रवेशः **श्री भवगुप्तराजदेव** विज्ञप्त्या **श्रीपुरतल** वास्तब्य (व्य) तैत्तिरि-

१२. **य भारद्वाजसगोत्रास्यां भट्ट भवदेव जनार्दनास्यां** सहोदर भ्रातृस्यां

१३. **चैत्र पौर्ण्णमास्यां** सोमग्रहोपरागे । उदकपूर्व्व मातापित्रोरात्मनश्च पू (पु)-

१४. ण्याभिबृ (वृ) द्धये ताम्र[८५] शासनेना चान्द्राक्र्कसमकालोपभोगार्थ प्रतिपादित

Second Plate : Reverse side (Plate-XVII)

१५. इत्यवगत्यानयो विधेयतय (या) समुचितं भोग भागादिक मू (मु) पन यद्भिः

१६. तवद्भिः[८६] सूचं[८७] प्रतिवस्तब्य (व्य) मिति ।। भाविनश्च भूमिपालानुदिश्ये दमभि-

१७. धि (धी) यते भूमिप्रदादिविल्ललं (ल) न्ति पतं (त) न्ति हं (ह) न्त **हत्वा महां (ही)** नृपतयो नरके नृ-

१८. शङ्गात्[८८] एतद्व (द्द्व) यं परिकलस्य (य्य) चलाञ्च लक्ष्मीमायुस्तथा कू (कु) **रूत**

१९. यद्भवतामभि (भी) ष्टं (।। १ ।।*) **अपि च (।*)** रक्षा पालनयोस्तावत्फलं **सुगति दुर्ग्गती** कोना-

२०. म स्वर्ग्ग मुच्छ्रूज्य नरकं प्रतिपद्यते ।। **(२ ।।*) ब्या (व्या) सगीतांश्चात्रश्लोकानुदाहरं (र) न्ति** (।*) .

२१. अज्ने (ग्ने) रपत्यं प्रथमं सुवर्ण्ण ाूर्व्वैष्णवि (वी) सूरूर्य सुताश्च गावः दत्तात्र-

Third Plate (Plate-XVIII)

२२. यस्तेन भवंन्ति[८९] लोकायः काञ्चनं गाञ्च महीञ्च दद्यात्।। ३ ।।* ष-

२३. ष्टि वर्ष सहस्त्रा (स्त्रा) णि स्वर्ग्गे मोदति भूमिदः आच्छेता चानुमन्ताचता-

२४. न्श्रयेव नरके वसेत ।। (४ ।।*) बहुभिर्वसुधा दत्ता राजभिः सगरादिभिः

२५. यस्य यस्य यदा भूमि तस्य तस्य तदा फलं (।। ५ ।।*) स्वदत्तां पर-

२६. दत्ताम्बायत्नाद्रक्ष युधिष्ठिर मही महिमतां श्रेष्ठ दानाश्रेयोनुपा-

२७. लनमिति ।। (६ ।।*) **श्री महाशिवगुप्त** राज देवस्य प्रवर्द्धमान **विजयराज्ये स**-

२८. **म्ब (म्व) त्सरे एकोनविङ्शतिमे** चैत्र दिनत्रिङ्शति आङ्केनापिसम्ब९० **१९ चैत्र दिन र्ल**

Mudra

०१. राज्ञ (:) श्री हर्षगुप्तस्य सूनो (:) सद्गुणशालिन (:)

०२. शासनं शिवगुप्तस्य सिथतमाभुवन स्थिते (।।*)

Acknowledgements

The present excavations at Sirpur are being conducted by Śrī A.K. Sharma, Archaeological Advisor, Govt. of Chhattisgsrh, under the aegis of Directorate, Culture and Archaeology, Govt. of Chhattisgsrh. I am grateful to the excavator for allowing me to write on these recently discovered copper plates. I am also thankful to the Directorate, Culture and Archaeology for giving me opportunity to work at Sirpur.

REFERENCES AND NOTES

* Originally not present but suggested.

0. Correct form of the incorrect word and letter.

1. These plates were recovered on 05/11/2008, from the area of SRP - 30 (Al, Qd- 2; Depth- 2. 27m, Layer- 6), mound located in between the Gandharveśvara temple and Rāyakerā pond at Sirpur bringing to light remains of township.
2. This grant was issued just eighty days after issuing of Rājim-Plates of the same king, in the same regnal year.
3. Shastri, A. M., 1995, *Inscriptions of Śarabhapurīyas, Pāṇḍuvamśīns and Somavamśīns,* II, p. 103-106.
4. *Ibid,* p. 107-111.
5. *Mahākosala Historical Society Papers,* II, p. -9.
6. For detail see: *IŚPS,* II, p. -105, fn-20a.
7. Means thirteenth day of bright fortnight of Pauṣa (*Pauṣa śuklapakṣa trayodasi)* beacause Pāṇḍuvamśīns calendar starts with dark fortnight and ends on *pūrṇimā* See: *IŚPS,* vol.-I, p. 380.
8. His Boṇḍā and Balodā plates, belonging to fifth and ninth regnal years were engraved by *akṣaśālika* (goldsmith) Boppanāga. He might have also inscribed Rājim plates and present inscription because both were issued at the same time but due to omission or oversight his naem is not recorded.
9. *CII,* IV, p. -421
10. *Ibdi,* p. -420.
11. From original specimen.
12. Expressed by a symbol.
13. Read 'निशितनिस्त्रिङ्श'

14. Read 'इवाकृतकरोद्वेग'
15. Read 'सम्पत्'
16. Read 'प्राक्तने'
17. Read 'गूढोगाढं'
18. Read 'स्वामी'
19. Read 'कुतृष्णोपि'
20. Read 'धर्मार्जनेन'
21. Correct form should be 'मषिदेवोपाध्याय'
22. Rajim plates- 'इत्यवगम्य' ; see: *IŚPS,* I, p.-109.
23. Here *amusvāra is redundant.*
24. Rajim plates- 'सुखम्प्रतिवस्तव्यमिति' ; see *IŚPS,* I, p.- 109.
25. Read 'ललन्ति'
26. Read 'एतद्वय'
27. Read 'महींमहींमतां'
28. It should be 'संवत्सरे'
29. *EI,* XXVII, pp. 287-91.
30. Shastri, II, p. 127.
31. *EI,* XXVII, pp. -319-325.
32. Shastri,vol. -II, p. 136.
33. Singh, Rahul Kumar and G.L. Rayakawar, *'Mahāśivagupta Bālārjuna ke samya kā Sirpur se Prāpt 9 tāmralekha nidhi'* in **B. C. Jain** (ed.) *Utkīrṇa Lekha,* Raipur, 2005, pp. 196-217.
34. People attending worship of Śiva.
35. An epithet of Śiva.
36. The grant of Mallāra copper-plates (undated) was also given on the same occasion. See *Utkīrṇa Lekha,* p. 46.
37. The charter was issued just next day after making the grant.
38. *Utkīrṇa Lekha,* p. 208.
39. *IŚPS,* II, p. 257f.
40. Sahu, N.K., A new survey of history of South-Kosala. New aspects of history of Orissa, p. 15.
41. *CII, K* V, p. 107.

42. *EI,* XII, p. 40.
43. From original specimen.
44. Expressed by a symbol.
45. Read 'सूनु':
46. Here *anusvāra* is redundant. Read 'सुवर्ण'
47. Here *visarga* is superfluous.
48. Read 'भूमिदः'
49. Here *visarga* is superfluous.
50. Here *visarga* is superfluous.
51. See above reference no. 3 and 5.
52. *Utkīrṇa Lekha,* p. 197 and 211.
53. *Ibid,* p. 201 and 204.
54. *IHQ,* XIX, pp. 139-46.
55. *Utkīrṇa Lekha,* p. 204.
56. From original specimen.
57. Expressed by a symbol.
58. Read 'कार्त्तिकेय'
59. Read 'सूनुः'
60. Here *visarga* is superfluous.
61. This punctuation mark is superfluous.
62. Other Sirpur grants of Mahāśivagupta- 'समाज्ञापयति'
63. Other Sirpur grants of Mahāśivagupta- 'सर्व्वपीडा'
64. Read 'मुच्छ्रिज्य'
65. Read 'भूर्व्वैष्णवी'
66. Read 'गाश्च महीश्च'
67. Read 'दद्यात्'
68. Read 'आक्षेप्ता'
69. *EI,* XXXIII, p. 60.
70. Nigam, L. S., 1998, *Dakṣina Kosala kā aitihāsika bhūgola,* Delhi, p. 162.
71. *Ibid,* p. -111.
72. Ali, S.M., 1971, *The geography of Purāṇas,* 2nd ed., p. 113.

73. *Utkīrṇa Lekha,* p. 45.
74. *Ibid,* p. 201.
75. *Ibid,* p. 213
76. *Ibid,* p. 211.
77. *IŚPS,* II, pp. 138-40.
78. *Ibid,* p. 167, 383; *EI, III,* pp. 340, 44.
79. *Ibid,* I, p. 172.
80. From original specimen.
81. Expressed by a symbol.
82 Here *anusvāra* is displaced read 'सम्पत्संपादित'
83. Read 'सूनुः'
84. Read 'सनिधि:'
85. Read 'ताम्र'
86. Read भवद्भिः'
87. Read 'सुखं'
88. Read 'नृशंसा:'
89. Hera *anusvara* is superfluous.
90. Read 'अङकेनापिसम्वत्'

3

BLACK COTTON SOIL AND EARLY FARMING CULTURE OF MALWA REGION

—*Dr. Pushp Lata Singh*

Malwa region (27°70'-25°10' N and 73°45'-79°14' E) is the western part of the present state of Madhya Pradesh with the Vindhyan Range on its North and the Satpura Range on its south. It has an area of 196,700 sq. km which is spread in 530 km in length and 390 km in width. It forms a distinct geographical unit by its physiography, economy, culture and environment. Situated in the heart of India, it includes all the land between the Vindhyas and a point just south of Gwalior. Its eastern limit is marked by a ridge which goes from south to north near Vidisha, While its, western limit lies near east of Aravalli Range in Rajasthan. It forms a link between the Indo-Gangetic plain in the north and the peninsular India in the south. It is located on the northern and southern tip of the great Malwa plateau. Two great river systems, the Narmada and the Chambal, irrigate the region. Malwa region is drained in its southern part by the Narmada, Tapi and Mahi which join the Gulf of Khambhat in Arabian sea, and Betwa in north which joins Yamuna of Indo-Gangetic Plain. The climate is of the tropical monsoon type, with its high fertility and the days are warm while nights are generally cool. The annual precipitation ranges around 1000 mm and therefore, the region has good vegetation cover.

The soil on the upper part of the surface of the Earth's crust that provides a medium for plant growth which is a complex and dynamic assemblage of components : rock particles of varying sizes, derived from weathering of the parent rock, humus, minerals in solution in water, air, and organisms including bacteria, arthropods and worms. Its formation, exact composition and physical and chemical properties depend on the interaction of geological, climate and biological factors. Albit, the origin and growth of soils, however, is a subject of great complexity involving a long series of changes ending in the production of clay-factor and other colloids of the soil. In Indian context they are either the altered residue of the underlying rocks, after the soluble constituents have been removed, mingled with some proportion of decomposed organic matter (residual soil) or the soilcap may be due to deposition of alluvial debris brought down by rivers from the higher altitude (driftsoil). The Indian residual soil differ markedly from the soils of European countries, which are largely of postglacial growth and in which the pedogenic process have not been in operation long enough to mature them, while the residual soil of India have close affinities with their rocky substratum, both as regards composition and morphology. Thus podsolisation is a common character of residual soil whose best example in Indian context are laterite and black cotton soil of Peninsular India. In contrast to it alluvial soils of the vast Indo-Gangetic plains, likewise differ from Peninsular soils and from the majority of European soils, in having undergone but little pedogenic evolution since their deposition by rivers so late as in sub-recent times and they are still largely immature and have not developed any characteristic soil profile.

The black cotton soil is a clayey to loamy residual soil composed largely of clay material and is spread almost in whole of the above cited region. The free calcium carbonate are invariably present at different depths of the soil profile. Cracks develop in summer season and in deep clayey soil they are even a meter or more deep. This soil is usually ill supplied with phosphate (P_2O_5), nitrogen and organic matter by the process of nitrogenase (bacterial fixation of nitrogen) but is sufficient in potassium felspar ($KALSi_3O_8$) and lime (CaO). The black colour of the soil is due to iron in the forms of magnetite (Fe_30_4) or to some minute quantity of a titanium iron compound i.e. ilmenite ($FeTi\ 0_3$), partly to carbon and organic matter (humus) with their residual nature of basaltic organic *in situ,* which is a type of igneous rock of volcanic origin which are characterised by high silica (SiO_2) content (45-50%). Here the residual nature means the soil derived *insitu* from the rocks present underneath of the same area by the process of weathering, depending by temperature effects, winds, precipitation, living agent and chemical action.

The thickness of the soil profile is highly variable from 30 cm to 15 m, and their composition shows considerable variation with different depth horizons, especially in its clay content and lime segregation. The clay is very rich in silica, 60% and 25% of alumina with only 15% of iron. The chemical composition of 84% black soil in Malwa region indicate high percentage of potassium, 54.5% are high in phosphorus, while 18% soils are low to medium in nitrogen, phosphoric acid and organic matter, but potash (K_2CO_3), lime (CaO) and iron (Fe_3O_4) contents are usually high. The nitrogen content of the soil is very low (0.02% to 0.05%), with high phosphoric acid (0.08 to 0.2%) potash (0.8 to 0.15%) and lime (1.0 to 7.7%)[1]. The texture of the soil is somewhat calcareous with very fine grain which is extremely sticky when wetted and has a capacity for retaining a large proportion of its moisture for a long time. It supported agriculture in the yore without measuring or being left fallow, and with no apparent sign of exhaustion or impoverishment.

In the Malwa region this soil has three sub types :

(a) Deep black soil.

(b) Medium black soil.

(c) Shallow black soil

Deep black soil covers major parts of the Narmada Valley (22^{0} 11'ṣ 22^{0} 40'; 75^{0} 36'-81^{0}45') and route of Vindhyan and Satpura plateau especially in the area of Hoshangabad. This soil may further be sub divided as black, dark brown, coarse brown, which is mixed and sandy. Though highly productive black soil in this part are known as *Mariar* and *Kabar*, they have clay content of 50-60% and calcium carbonate of 0.45%. The pH value ranges from 7 to 7.5. Medium black soil covers major portion of the region including Sagar, Nimar (East and West), Raisen, Sehore etc. and is suitable for most of the rabi crops. The soils of Sagar, Mandsaur and Shajapur contain 20-40% clay while in Vidisa, Guna, Indore, Dhar, Ujjain and Dewas districts it varies from 30 to 35%. The shallow black soil is spread over the region of Satpura Ridge, Betul, Jhabua, Jhalwar, West Ratlam, Mandsaur and Banswara. It consists of shallow loams having 15-30% clay. The important types are dark brown clay, loamy rich soil, black soil and poor light hilly soil. This soil is comparatively less productive.

The black cotton soil plays a pivotal role in the development of early farming cultures of India, which was formed during the early part of Holocene. It attracted and prompted early farming people due to its high fertility index and optimal pH value for growing dry farming cereals. As far as evidence reveals the first settlers of this land, who used pottery were the chalcolithic people. The possibility of Neolithic settlements are not altogether ruled out. According to Khare[2], the Rangai (23°42'; 79°14') excavation yielded Neolithic greyware which was a part of chalcolithic complex. Similar type of greyware with Neolithic celts were unearthed in the Eran (24°5'; 78°10') excavations from the chalcolithic level in the same plateau of Malwa. Here Eran is situated on the south bank of the river Bina (ancient Venva), a tributary of Betwa (Vetravati) on which Rangai was situated, means both were well connected during Neolithic period.

So far as settlement pattern of the chalcolithic culture is concerned, settlements like Navdatoli (22°11'; 75°36'), Pipliya-Lorka (23°40'; 79°13') and Eran (24°5'; 78°10') etc. were located on the deep black to medium black cotton soil zone. But there is no trace of chalcolithic settlements in the shallow black cotton soil zone because this soil was not much suitable for cultivation of rabi crops. Albeit there is only two chalcolithic settlements i.e. Awara (24°8'; 75°30') and Manoti (24°10'; 75°42') which were located in Mandsaur district in the shallow black cotton soil zone. Over 40 settlements of Kaytha (2400-2100 B.C.) and 100 settlements of the Malwa culture (1800-1500 B.C.) have been reported in the black cotton area of Malwa region. Here the Kaytha culture located mostly in the Chambal valley while Malwa lying between the Chambal in the north and Narmada in the south i.e. between the 25° and 19° N parallels and the 73° and 78° E longitudes. The studies have shown that the widespread chalcolithic culture in the area of the valleys of Chambal, Narmada, Betwa and other rivers were frequently colonized by the people in a period from about 2000 B.C. to 600 B.C.[3]

Kaytha	(23°14'; 76°2')	-	Choti Kali Sindh Valley
Runija	(23°20'; 76°10')	-	Melani and its tributary Valley
Nagda	(23°42'; 75°47')	-	Lower Chambal Valley
Awara	(24°8'; 75°30')	-	Lower Chambal Valley
Dangwada	(23°16'; 75°12')	-	Lower Chambal Valley
Gilaulikhera	(24°12'; 75°47')	-	Chambal Valley (Kumari River)
Eran	(24°5'; 78°10')	-	Bina (a tributary of Betwa)
Rangai	(23°42'; 79°14')	-	Bina (a tributary of Betwa)
Pipliya-Lorka	(23°40'; 79°13')	-	Kaliyaso : a tributary of Betwa
Maheshwar	(22°11'; 75°36')	-	Narmada Valley
Tripuri	(23°16'; 80°13')	-	Narmada Valley
Kakarehata	(22°46'; 77°12')	-	Narmada Valley
Mahidpur	(22°12'; 75°52')	-	Shipra river Valley

The aforementioned chalcolithic settlements evince that in the Malwa region the early settlements located in the tributaries of Chambal, Betwa and Narmada not in the main rivers which is often subjected to high floods is evident from its high banks. Navdatoli is some 30 m in height from present bed of Narmada; the southern and the northern banks naturally afforded protection from floods and hence large chalcolithic settlements flourished here for half a millennium in the past. But on the main river the habitation is away at about 2-3 km from its banks. In the Chambal river, the settlements are quite small, not more than a couple of hectares in extent. The Chambal river has developed deep ravines during late quarterny period, and the region was not fit for human habitation. The people of chalcolithic culture, therefore, avoided such areas for habitation.

Settled life in the Malwa region began around the beginning of the second millennium with the Kaytha culture horizon, dated, at the type site of Kaytha ($23^{0}14'$; $76^{0}2'$) in Ujjain district, from as early as 2000 B.C. to 1800 B.C. Subsequently, the region was flourished by the Banas (1700 B.C.-1500 B.C.), and Malwa cultures (1700-1500 B.C.). The excavated chalcolithic settlements of the Malwa region are as follows:

Site		District
Kaytha[4]	($23^{0}14'$; $76^{0}2'$)	Ujjain
Nagda[5]	($23^{0}42'$; $75^{0}47'$)	Ujjain
Mahidpur[6]	($22^{0}12'$; $75^{0}52'$)	Ujjain
Runija[7]	($23^{0}20'$; $76^{0}10'$)	Ujjain
Dhangwada[8]	($23^{0}2'$; $76^{0}6'$)	Ujjain
Awara[9]	($24^{0}8'$; $75^{0}30'$)	Mandsaur
Manoti[10]	($24^{0}12'$; $75^{0}52'$)	Mandsaur
Jharda[11]	($24^{0}16'$; $75^{0}16'$)	Mandsaur
Maheshwar[12]	($22^{0}11'$; $75^{0}36'$)	West Nimar
Navdatoli[13]	($22^{0}11'$; $75^{0}36'$)	West Nimar
Eran[14]	($24^{0}5'$; $78^{0}10'$)	Sagar
Kakarehata[15]	($23^{0}37'$; $80^{0}2'$)	Jabalpur
Tripuri[16]	($23^{0}16'$; $80^{0}36'$)	Jabalpur

Pipliya Lorka[17]	($23^0 40'; 79^0 13'$)	Raisen
Besnagar[18]	($23^0 32'; 77^0 48'$)	Vidisa
Rangai[19]	($23^0 36'; 77^0 16'$)	Vidisa
Gilaulikhera[20]	($26^0 32'; 78^0 11'$)	Moreina
Azadnagar[21]	($22^0 42'; 75^0 56'$)	Indore
Mandsaur	($22^0$4E'; $75^0$7'N)	Mandsaur

These above chalcolithic settlements were vertically associated with different cultural horizons of the chalcolithic period which is given below :

Site		Cultural Horizon
Kaytha	-	Kaytha+Ahar+Malwa
Nagda	-	Kaytha+Malwa
Mahidpur	-	Kaytha+Malwa+Late Harappan
Runija	-	Kaytha
Dhangwada	-	Kaytha+Ahar+Malwa+Late Harappan
Awara	-	Ahar+Kaytha+Malwa
Manoti	-	Ahar+Kaytha+Malwa+Late Harappan
Maheshwar	-	Kaytha+Malwa
Navdatoli	-	Ahar+Malwa+Jorwe+Late Harappan
Eran	-	Kaytha+Malwa
Mandsaur	-	Kaytha Ware
Kakarehata	-	Malwa
Tripuri	-	Malwa
Pipliya Lorka	-	Kaytha+Malwa
Besnagar	-	Kaytha
Jharda	-	Kaytha+Ahar+Malwa
Rangai	-	Kaytha+Malwa

Gilaulikhera	-	Malwa
Azadnagar	-	Kaytha + Late Harappan

The earliest settlers of Kaytha[23] people (2000-1800 B.C.) were using chocolate slipped ware called as Kaytha ware associated with red painted buff ware and combed ware. All the Kaytha settlements were considerably small, extending not more than 2 hectare in extent. They are usually located on the tributaries of Chambal and Betwa.

Although the Banas culture[24] was mainly concentrated in the region of Banas river plain of south-east Rajasthan but some of its traits like the black-and-red ware had been noticed at sites like Navdatoli, Kaytha, Awara and Manoti in the Malwa region of Madhya Pradesh. The culture as represented in Central India has two additional traits which are not well represented in Rajasthan. As against the paucity of stone tools at sites like Ahar, Kaytha has produced a full fledged lithic blade industry which was developed due to the paucity of copper ore in Central India. The second feature is the rich number of terracotta figurines made of fine clay, baked at consistently high temperature so as avoid blotchy surface. The author of this culture probably lived in simple houses similar to that of Banas culture. This confirms that the Banas/Ahar culture was clearly oriented towards the Malwa plateau on the one hand and Gujarat on the other where black soil pre-existed. The presence of Banas lavel at Kaytha and of the Ahar ceramics at a number of sites in the Malwa region underlines the closeness of this interaction. As it unfolded and flowered into a major chalcolithic phenomenon known as the Malwa culture, it embraced the plains of a large number of rivers that intersect the area such as the Chambal, Ken, Kali Sindh, Mahi, Sipra and the Narmada. Thus the Malwa plateau was the corridor through which various routes of south-east Rajasthan move further down towards Maharashtra. From the Malwa plateau, there developed, possibly very early, a route going across the Narmada to the central Tapti basin in Maharashtra. This is confirmed by the presence of Kaytha ware at Kaothe (21°56'; 74°15') in Dhule district. It is, however, the Malwa phase which marks the high point of interaction along this route in the period prior to the early historic phase when, along with Malwa, shell and coral also came to be included in the artefactual repertoires of important centers in the more southern sites like Prakash (21°30'; 74°21') and Nevasa (19°34'; 74°54') in Maharashtra. The affinites with Maharashtra were equally close although, by the Jorwe period (1500-1050 B.C.), the region became more southward oriented. But what is equally, if not more, interesting is the presence of the late Harappans in Malwa. Lustrous red ware has been reported at Dangwada (23°16'; 75°12') in lower Chambal valley and other explored sites also draw attention to some new late Harappan sites in this region. Much earlier Wakankar in 1982 found in the lowest levels of Manoti ($24^0$12'; $75^0$52') elongated Harappan jars, dish-on-stand and beaded necked storage jars. Among the more interesting developments in the study of the chalcolithic cultures in Malwa is the evidence of fire-altars and perhaps temples at Dangwada which has also yielded evidence of bull and phallus worship in its chalcolithic stage.

The populace of the Malwa culture were not only attracted and flourished on the black cotton soil due to its optimum fertility index but instead they were attracted and thrived owing to the favourable eco-scenario system too e.g. Navdatoil, which has hills on north and south with the vast expanse of the Narmada in between. The site covers an area of 10 hectare which is one of the largest chalcolithic settlement in the country. Like Navdatoli, Eran[25] and Nagda[26] are in the same ecogeographical horizon. Although the first mentioned site is the largest, the other two also appear to be important settlements as they are said to have been fortified. The remaining settlements of the Malwa culture are small in extent ranging from 1 to 4 hectare. Therefore, a sort of two level settlement pattern, consisting of small and large is the premier feature of Malwa culture. Small villages are too many to enumerate, among the larger ones, Navdatoli, Nagda and Eran may be incorporated. The Kaytha settlements indicate a random pattern while the Malwa sites appear to be somewhat clustered around such regional centres as Nagda, Eran and Navdatoli where the Malwa ware is the dominant fabric of the ceramic industry. It is a buff or orange-slipped ware painted in black or dark brown. A thinner and fine variety of it occurring in abundance at Eran has been called Eran fabric. The repertoire of painted designs is extremely rich and consists of over 600 motifs. These are both geometrical and naturalistic in character. The culture is truly chalcolithic in character on account of the use of both copper and stone.

Soil and Farming

The black soil had immense potentiality of dry farming for rabi crops only and not for Kharif crops due to its optimum pH value which is 7 to 8. In contrast to it investigation of the soil regions of the megalithic areas in Peninsular India and Sri Lanka, the yellowish-brown soil is unsuitable for dry farming of rabi crops due to low water retention (high sand content does not encourage water retention) low wiloing point (as a consequence of low water retention wiloing point is reached fairly rapidly) and high acidity of soil during the rainy season as minerals such as ferrous, magnesium and sodium are leached out to a lower horizon. Under drier conditions these minerals surface and get deposited at the very upper horizon, consequently, this makes the soil very acidic. The pH value of this soil type is lower than 7. It suggests that the early iron age people selected area of this soil type, which is unsuitable for agricultural purposes, for erection of megaliths. On the contrary the Gangetic basin have low pH value, but is good for early farming settlers due to its high wiloing point.

The black soil played a vital role in determining the settlement and subsistence pattern of the early farming communities in Central and Western India who were mostly practising dry farming (farming without artificial irrigations). But our knowledge of the chalcolithic farming is still shady and sketchy owing to the fact that sufficient attention was not paid by excavators for the recovery of grains during excavation in the area. The evidence of archaeobotanical remains have been reported from the sites of Kaytha[27], Navdatoli, Dhangwada[28] and Mahidpur only. Navdatoli is the sole exception of chalcolithic settlement in the Malwa region which have provided excellent palaeobotanical evidences which confirm that the author of the chalcolithic cultures were farmers although they subsisted on hunting and fishing too. The climate (rainfall 400-1000 mm per annum) of the Malwa region was also suitable for various rabi crops. Malwa also gets winter rains and hence wheat and barley could have been easily grown there. The early farming people of the Kaytha culture had cultivated two kinds of wheat (*Triticum sphaerococcum* and *Triticum compactum*), horse gram (*Dolichos biflours linn*) and Linseed.

Other sites i.e. Dangwada and Mahidpur[29] have also yielded important evidence of archaeobotanical remains. In all 13 samples of carbonized seeds ranging in age from chalcolithic to the early historical period of Dangwada were studied. Food grains identified from chalcolithic period are of *Oryza rufipogon* (wild rice), *Oryza Sativa* (cultivated rice). *Triticum aestivum*, *Vigna mungo*, *Vigna radiatus*, *Lens esculentus*, etc. Dangwada excavation also revealed carbonized grains of barley in Period I. The charred food grains like Jawari (a kind of millet) and Mung (a kind of legumes) have been reported from Mahidpur. Burnt grains of rice were found at KTH-5 at Kayatha[32] which is the earliest evidence of rice cultivation in Malwa. The charred grains of rice were also found from other sites like Tripuri. Navdatoli comprises the remains of cereals, oil seeds and legumes which is as follows :

A. Cereals

Wheat : Charred or carbonized grains of wheat were found in all the phases. Vishnu Mittre[31] distinguishes mainly two kinds :

(a) **Bread wheat :** The grains are short, oblong, grooved and thick with their ends broad and blunt. Identified as *Triticum vulgare compactum*, which is different from the spelt and emmer wheats.

(b) **Bread wheats with pointed ends :** Comparable to spelt in shape, but their L/B and T/B ratios are different, and therefore regarded as a variety of or nearer to the wheat of the first type.

Barley : Barley had also been found in the excavations but for some reasons it was missed during the earlier studies. Later, Dr. Kajale, while restudying the old collections, has found charred barley grains as well. In fact, this was expected, when a site like Inamgaon ($18^{0}35'$; $74^{0}30'$)had yielded barley grains from the Malwa level.

Rice : It was absent in Phase I, but present in Phase II-IV. The grains are oblong, flattened on the sides and strongly ribbed. It is identified as a variety of *Oryza sativa L.*

B. Legumes

Lentil : Found in all the phases. The grains are thick and lenticular in shape with the keel edge preserved in some. Identified as Lens *culinaris Medikus* (*Lens esculenta Moench*).

Black Gram (Urd) : The seeds are square or oblong with a pronounced concaved hylum scar, and said to resemble the black or dark brown-seeded variety. Identified as *Phaseolus mungo L.* Probably this is the earliest find in India.

Green Gram (Mung) : The seeds are square to roundish and smaller than those of Urd. The hylum scare with a raised ridge visible in some identified as *Phaseolus radiates L.* and probably it is the first occurrence in India.

Seeds of four other leguminous weeds also occur :

Pisum arvense L.

Lathyrus sphaericus Retz.

Vicia sativa Linn

V. tetrasperma Moench

C. Oil Seeds

Linseed : Found in Phase I, III and IV of Navdatoli in a pure, unmixed form. The seeds are well preserved with a distinct beak at the micro-pylar end.

Identified as *Linum usitatissimuin Linn.*, it is now extensively cultivated in India for extracting oil and not for making flax. Presumably this was also in use at Navadatoli.

Grass Pea : The seeds are very much compressed and wedge-shaped with the small hilum on one side of the thick end. Identified as *Lathyrus sativus Linn.*

The people of the Malwa culture cultivated the above crops in the alluvial tracts of the Narmada, Chambal and their tributaries; but they might have also cultivated in the rich black cotton soil for which Malwa is famous. The black cotton soil which had immense potentiality for the production of varied crops was focus of attraction for the early farming populace. Its nutral (pH-7) to slightly alkaline (pH-8) feature, which is an ideal situation for optimal fertility of the soil. It has been suggested that the chalcolithic farmers might have used a wooden plough as some farmers do in parts of Madhya Pradesh where wood of Khair (*Acacia catechu*) is presently used in the hard, compact black soil. Here Khair wood is 5.76 hard on Moh's scale of hardness to diamond which is 10 on Mohs scale. Although there is no evidence forthcoming of plough from the excavated Malwa site so far.

It has been observed that the black soil of Malwa does process the swelling feature of the soil due to high content of *montmorillonite* and *beidellite* groups of clay minerals by which is sticky when wet and has a capacity for retaining a large proportion of moisture for a long time but when it dries up it has cracks due to losing the inherent moisture content. This, according to Lishnik, "Clearly represents ecological adaptation dictated by available technology, knowledge and means. An analogy with the present day agricultural methods in these regions lead to the supposition or that we are dealing here with a system of dry-farming, dependent on moisture retentive soil."[33] Wallace had opined that "the soil has wonderful power of absorbing water, cultivation can be practiced even without the availability of irrigation facilities".[34] It is said that "the black cotton soil ploughs itself." Thus we gather from the settlement scenario of the cited soil in Malwa region that in the yore had constantly influenced the human settlement due to its rich loamy earth possessing unusual power to retain moisture and on account of its agricultural prosperity and the role it has played as a route to west India and the Deccan from the Indo-Gangetic plain. On account of all these Malwa has always been considered a significant geo-poletico-economic and cultural region in Early Indian history.

REFERENCES

1. Wadia, D.N.; *Geology of India* (London, 1953), 48-49.

2. *Prachya Pratibha*, Vol. 1, No. 2 (Bhopal, 1976), 38-43.

3. Wakankar, V.S.; Chalcolithic Culture of Malwa, *Prachya Pratibha*, Vol. I, No. 2 (Bhopal, 1976), 14-16.

4. *Indian Archaeology-A Review*, 1964-65 : 32-33; Wakankar, V.S. *Kaytha Excavation Report* (Ujjain, 1967), Vikram University,5-16.

5. *IAR*, 1955-56, 11.

6. Ali, Rahman (Delhi, 2004) *Chalcolothic Site of Ujjain Region, Mahidpur* (Excavation Report).

7. Brief cyclostyled Report on Runija Excavation, Archaeology and Museum, Bhopal.

8. Singh, R.P. : *Puratan*, Vol. No. 2 and 3 (Bhopal, 1984), 83-86. *Excavations at Dangwada*, 1983. *Puratan*, Vol. I, 104-108.

9. *IAR*, 1956-57, 5; 1958-59, 27; 1959-60, 22.

10. *IAR*, 1959-60, 20.

11. Wakankar, V.S; (Kurukshetra, 1976) in *Archaeological Congress and Seminar*, 1972, 22-40.

12. Sankalia, H.D.; Subbarao. B. and Deo, S.B.; *Excavations at Maheshwar and Navdatoil*, 1952-53 (Poona and Baroda, 1958), 65-70.

13. Ansari, Z.D. and Dhavalikar, M.K. *World Archaeology*, No. 3 (London, 1972), 337-45 and *Excavation at Kayatha* (Pune, 1975), 36-51.

14. Bajpai, K.D.; '*Sagar Through the Ages*', (Sagar, 1965), 26-31; *New Light on the Early History of Central India*, Singh, U.V. *Eran-A Chalcolithic settlement*; *Bulletin of A.I.H.C. and Archaeology*, Sagar University, Vol. I (Sagar, 1967), 29-38; Pandey, S.K. *Prachya Pratibha*, Vol. 1, No. 2 (Bhopal, 1976), 54-61.

15. Sharma, R.K.; *Excavation at Kakerhata* (1984-85), Prof. K.D. Bajpai Felicitation, Vol. I, 63-67; *Excavation at Kakerhata* (Rupnath), (Delhi, 1992), 71-72.

16. Dixit, M.G.; *Tripuri*, 1952 (Nagpur, 1955), 13-14.

17. Tiwari, S.; *Chalcolithic Culture of the Betwa source region*, *Prachya Pratibha*, (Bhopal, 1976), Vol. IV, No. 2, pp. 77-80; Krishna, C.; Pipliya-Lorka Excavations (Brief Report), *Puratana*, Vol. I, No. 2-3, 1984, pp. 87-91.

18. Khare, M.D.; Chalcolithic remains from Besnagar, *Prachya Pratibha*, Vol. IV, No. 2 (Bhopal 1976), 38-42; *IAR,* 1963-64, 64-65 and 1965-66; Singh U.V.; Proto History Pottery of Eastern Malwa (Ph.D. Thesis, 1966), 52-65.

19. *IAR*, 1975-76; Khare, M.D. (Bhopal, 1976) op.cit., 42-43.

20. Sharma, R.K.; Excavations at Gilauli Khera 1982; *Prachya Pratibha,* Vol. IX-X (Bhopal, 1981-82), 5-9; Mishra, C.B.; Some problems of chalcolithic cultures of Central India, *Prachya Pratibha*, Vol. X-XI (Bhopal, 1982-83), 119-121.

21. Wakankar, V.S., 1976 in *Archaeological Congress and Seminar,* 1976 (Kurukshetra), 24-25.

22. Sharma, R.K.; *Indian Archeology, New Perspectives* (Delhi, 1982), 198-199.

23. Ansari, Z.D. and Dhavalikar, M.K; *Excavations at Kaytha,* 1968 (Poone, 1975), 46-56.

24. Sankalia, H.D. Deo, S.B. and Ansari, Z.D; *Excavations at Ahar* (Tambavati), (Poone, 1969), 61-63; and Hooja, Rima; *The Ahar Culture* (Oxford, 1988), 25-40.

25. Singh, U.V., (Sagar, 1962), *op. cit.* 39-40.

26. *IAR*, 1955-56, p. 14.

27. Ansari, Z.D. and Dhavalikar, M.K. (Pune, 1975), *op. cit.* 54-56.

28. Singh, R.P. (1984), *op. cit.*

29. Ali, Rahman, *op. cit.*

30. Wakankar, V.S. and M.D. Khare; (Delhi, 1981), Dangwada excavation (Ujjain), *Malwa through the Ages* (eds.) M.D. Khare, pp. 92-95 and Wakankar V.S. *New Light on Central Indian Archacology Through Kayatha Excavations, Puratattva* No. 2 (Varanasi, 1969), 26-29.

31. *Technical Reports on Archeological Remains*, (Poone, 1961), 15-16.

32. Kajale, M.D; 1974, *Ancient grains from India*, 34, 35-75.

33. Leshnik, Lawrence S; 1968. *Prehistoric Exploration in North Gujrat and parts*

of Rajasthan, *East and West*, Vol. 18, (Rome : Is MEO, 1968), 295-310; *The system of dry farming in the West Nimad district of Central India*, *Year Book of the South Asia Institute*, (Heidelberg, 1967), 56-74.

34. Wallace, R; *India in 1887*, (Edinburg, 1888), 32-36 and Zeuner, F.E., *Report of the all-India soil survey scheme*, Indian Council of Agricultural Research Bulletin No. 73 (Delhi, 1953), 74-78.

* Reader, Deptt. of A.I.H.C. and Archaeology, B.H.U., Varanasi.

4

LEELAR : A MEGALITHIC IRON SMELTING CULTURE OF CHHATTISGARH

—*Professor Ashoka K. Mishra*

The literal meaning of megalithic is large stone (from the Greek *megas,* 'large' and *lithos,* 'stone'), is generally applied to monuments made of large stone-slabs including Chamber Tombs, Menhirs. Stone Circle and Alignments. In Indian context the megalithic builders seem to have been mainly rice agriculturists, and iron-users with black-and-red ware ceramic tradition. Recent works suggest that Indian megaliths were being built and used throughout most of the 1st millennium B.C. and into the first few century A.D. with the innovation of iron metallurgy which is the third age of three age system of classification as defined by the main material used for making tools by a Danish archaeologist Christian Thomsen in 1836. So iron metal and megalithic culture are the two sides of the same coin in Indian archaeology. The ore of iron occurs on a large scale where megalithic sites are found in India, chiefly in the form of hematite, laterite and magnetite. It prevails especially in the Peninsula where the crystalline and schistone rocks of the Dharwar and Guddapah system enclose at some places ferruginous deposits of an extraordinary magnitude.

In a scientific way almost all the metal on outer shell of the lithosphere (earth crust) is found combined with oxygen or sulphur in ores (a natural mineral of iron/ copper from which useful substances can be extracted) although small amounts of 'native' metal (*i.e.* found in nature uncombined with any other elements) do exist. Several millennia elapsed between the time when people learned about the properties of metals from these rare finds and the time when they learned how to smelt, that is to conduct the chemical reactions needed to liberate metals from their ores e.g. the red colour of haematite (Fe_2O_3), laterite ($Fe_2.O_3L_2$ $(OH)_4.Si_2O_5$) and black colour of magnetite ($Fe3O_4$) were used in prehistoric painting since *Circa* 35,000 B.C. during upper palaeolithic period, but iron was extracted from the same at about 2000 B.C. after a longer gap of about 30000 years. The rare deposits of free copper (0.56% of the earth crust) were probably discovered by the start of ninth millennium B.C. The next metal of which mankind had knowledge was gold in the form of electrum, an alloy of gold and silver containing 55-85% of gold (0.00 4% of the earth crust) which was scarce but meteoritic iron (4.2% the earth crust) which was in abundance but was discovered too late by the mankind due to its technical complexity of extraction from its ore. Since in the ancient times the iron smelting was technically very complex, therefore, it was costlier. to gold upto the beginning of Christian era. This fact is amply corroborated that while in the treaty concluded between Alexander the Great and Porus in 326 B.C.. Porus had given 30 lb or 13.608 Kg Indian steel to Alexander as gift which has been mentioned by Quntius Cuertius. In Roman records iron was known as *Ferrum indicum* means iron of India while in post medieval European records Indian steel was called as *wootz* means steel which contain 0.2 to 0.4% carbon. It is a very superior kind of steel exported to Europe, for manufacture of swords and other weapons. It testifies to the metallurgical skill of the early Indians. Here *wootz* is by origin a Kannad word *ukku* means steel[4] which was being made in India from late medieval period. It is made from direct reduction of iron ore by the process of charging of iron and vegetable matter in a sealed crucible under high temperature to be made by blowing air over charcoal. The *wootz* had lower carbon as cast iron have carbon level of 1.6%. which meant that the crucible temperature was at least in the range of 1400-1500° C during *wootz* manufacturing. Such a high temperature must be reached in a bellows-blown charcoal fire. In contrast to Indian *wootz,* the European iron cakes having high-carbon were probably forged at a not-too high temperature in the range of 650-850°C (between 'blood-red' 650°C to 'cherry-red 850°C) and then heat treated by quenching. Here quenching is the rapid cooling of metal by immersing it in bath of liquid in order to improve its properties. Iron is quenched to make them harder, but some nonferrous metals are quenched for other seasons, e.g. copper is made softer by quenching. The European smiths failed to reproduce the result, probably because they were familiar with low carbon steel having a higher melting point, and tried to forge *wootz* at a white heat, when the cementite phase dissolved in the austenite, and the brittle structure crumbled under the hammer. Heating and quenching produced martensitic structure providing additional hardness before 727°C and it would have been hard as well as tough (non-brittle). On the other hand, heating to much above 800°C before quenching would endow brittleness in the *wootz,* giving a bad reputation to Indian *wootz.* The rate of cooling of the iron ingot at various temperatures are critically important; the medieval smiths attributed magical properties to the quenching media such as blood, urine, milk, etc. which possessing different specific heat ensured different rates of cooling of the hot iron ingot. Although iron is the basic starting material for modern tools, wrought iron (which the Hittites made in Anatolia around 1700 B.C.) is relatively soft, so that knives swords and ploughshares of wrought iron will not hold their edge, but it easily gets shape and welded. It is fibrous and malleable and melted at 1500°C but softness in it started at about 1000°C which help in making structure etc. Due to this very fact, the Meharouli iron pillar of Delhi, Dhar pillar of Malwa and Iron beam of Lingraj (Bhuwanshwar) and Sun Temple of Korank were made of wrought iron which contain less than 0.05% corbon. In contrast to it, cast iron (alloy of iron, silica and 2.5 to 4% carbon) is very hard, so it is helpfull in tool making. In the case of grey cast iron the silica content is very high and carbon is in the graphitic form, while in the case of white cast iron, silica content is low and carbon is present in the cementite form (Fe_3C). The iron-carbon equilibrium state enable the internal structure of steel and cast iron to be tied with their chemical composition and cooling conditions. The microstructures obtained when steel specimens of various carbon content are cooled slowly, because steel have very low carbon content (0.02%) and consist ferrite alone. As the carbon content is increased, ? new structural constituent of iron-carbon alloys, pearlite is found. An increase in the carbon concentration in the steel leads a proportional increase in the amount of pearlite. The microstructure of iron-carbon alloys containing over 2% carbon, cast iron, depends not only upon their chemical composition but also upon the cooling rate in solidification of the liquid. In rapidly cooled molten cast iron the carbon may separate in the form of cementite disseminations embedded in the metal matrix. In white cast iron all of this is in the form of cementite i.e. the combined state. Here white cast irons are very brittle and hard. The smelting of iron was discovered and successfully accomplishing in the ancient time must forever remain a source of astonishment and admiration. The miraculous transformation of ore into metal is apparently accomplished solely by fire, and in sense it is, provided that ore understands by fire both heat and the carbon monoxide (CO) produced by burning charcoal; the carbon monoxide (CO) and carbondioxide (CO_2) in the ratio of 3:1 is essential for conversion of ore to metal (i.e. the reduction of iron oxide to the free iron metal). If this ratio was not maintained in the furnance, then metallic iron can not be obtained from its ore, whatever the temperature may be. To smelt iron ore, a furnance was charged with alternate layer of iron ore and charcoal (i.e. carbon), and in the smelting process carbon takes the oxygen away from the iron oxide to yield metallic iron and carbondioxide. Here charcoal is obtained by heating wood without air (dry distillation process), which contain 80% to 90% carbon, 10% to 18% moisture, 0.6% to 1.2% surlphur with calorific value of 6500 to 7500 K.cal per kg. So the charcoal used both as fuel and reducing agent. The sulphur of the charcoal is harmful in smelting, because it dissolves with extracted metal. Since sulphur is a very reactive non-metallic element of the oxygen group shows a wide range of oxidation numbers from +2 to +6, as is common with nonmetals but when it combined with metals like iron etc., it shows negative oxidation numbers commonly -2 as range of oxidation number of sulphur damage the properties of metallic iron, by reconverting it into its ore form. The compound of iron and iron sulphide ($Fe+FeS+Fe_2S3 + Fe_7S_8$) is known as eutectic. Here eutectic is a mechanical mixture of two substances shows a sharp melting point and the mixture is said to be a eutectic mixture and the temperature at which this occurs is called the eutectic temperature. Here in the case of iron and iron sulphide, the eutectic temperature of iron sulphide is 800° C while of pre-iron is 1200°C. means at 800° C this iron sulphide is in quasifluid state in the solid of iron. This quasifluid state of iron sulphide in solid state of iron is harmful to iron in the following ways:

(1) It reduces the tensile strength of the pure iron. Here tensile is defined as the stress expressed as the force per unit cross-sectional area, required to break it.

(2) It decreases the fatigue strength and breaks the metal if cylindrical loading is applied.

(3) The optimum strength of sulphur in in iron is 0.04% and if its percentage increases from its optimum phase, then iron is very brittle. If it is upto 0.04%, then it functions as anticorrison agent.

In this process charcoal cannot bring carbon atoms in contact with the oxygen atoms of iron ore, even if both the ore and the charcoal are crushed. Atoms are incredibly small (of the order of 0.00000005 cm in diameter), and chemistry occurs between atoms that are essentially in contact with one another. Two solids cannot be ground fine enough to bring their atoms into contact. Although smelting is something of a miracle. It is not miraculous enough to permit action at a distance; chemistry is an extremely intimate science, and action at a distance would be required if two solids were to react. But the reduction of iron ores does occur. What really happens ? The processes are as follows :

$$C + O_2 \rightarrow CO_2 \quad ....(1)$$

$$C + CO_2 \rightarrow 2CO \quad ....(2)$$

$$4CO + Fe_3O_4 \rightarrow 3Fe + 4CO_2 \quad ....(3)$$

Here the combustion of carbon to form carbon dioxide as reaction (1) is exothermic means heat is evolved by the reaction itself by which the temperature of smelting furnace increases upto 27%. As in reaction (2) the carbondioxide of reaction (1) again combined with carbon of the charcoal to form carbonmonoxide, so the percentage of carbon monoxide increases upto 70% in contrast to carbondioxide in lowerportion of the blast furnance which make the proper reducing atmosphere by which iron came out from its oxide ore as per above reaction (3).

A stream of air was forced into furnace with a bellows to supply oxygen called as blast furnace'. Some of the carbon burns in the stream of air to carbon dioxide, producing most of the heat needed to speed the process[6]. Then additional charcoal is attacked by the carbon dioxide to yield carbonmonoxide which reacts with the iron oxide to take away its oxygen from carbondioxide and leave the free metallic iron. No two solids need react with one another; it is gases that react with solids. The gas molecules are free to slop into the smallest interspaces of the solids, and so can react with buried atoms; reaction occurs at only minute distances. Gaseous oxygen and gaseous carbondioxide can both find the cracks in and react with solid charcoal and gaseous carbon monoxide can find and combine with the oxygen atoms in the solid iron ore.

The contextual Leelar (81°40" E Latitude, 20°39'40" N Longitude) is a megalithic site present in Dhamatri District of Chhattisgarh explored by Sri S.S. Yadava and Dr. Bharti Shrota of the State Arechaeology Department, Govt of Chhattisgarh. The 10 meter high mound of Leelar is present at the triangle of Mahanadi and a local rivulet Jharjhara. In trial trench of 2005-06, the excavator obtained BRW, pointed bone implement, iron arrow head and iron sickle, along with terracotta bead and half scotch. The bowls and dishes in BRW were made by well levigated clay on a very fast wheel. Leelar is a habitation site of the Megalithic culture and 2 Km. away from it the Megalithic. burial site is present at Aroud. Therefore, Leelar and Aroud are the best example of the burial and habitabional Megalithic site in the same vicinity. During my visit in the month of June, 2007 at the site I saw many Megalithic monuments in Dhamtari Distinict, when I was on way to Leelar, in the cultivated fields.

The region is based on Cuddapah[7] sedimentary platform and the Archean[8] granites and gneisses exposed in the basin and surrounding upland respectively. These flat to gently dipping sedimentary beds rest uncomformably on the Archaean granites and gneisses which is a type of metamorphic rock derived from the basin boundary at places, is formed by metamorphic rocks belonging to the Chilpighat series of the Dharwar System[9] sandwiched between the overlying Cuddapah beds and underlying Archaen granites and gneisses. The tropical red and yellow soil of the region developed *in situ* The red colour that prevails in the soils here is due to the diffusion of the iron contained in these underneath rocks of the area, by the process of laterization during Pleistocene phase. But here the process of laterization is not so marked as in the tropical rainforest climate of Kerla where it was first reported by Buchanan where blackish-red colour of it is formed due to deciduous forest, which results in significant humus in the soil profile of the lithosphere. The upper part of the soils show their deficiency of mineral like calcium magnesium, lime potash, which are more concentrated in the lower part of the soil profile of the region. The coarseness and low humus content of the soils explain their low fertility. These lateritic soils clearly show the development of some thick patches of laterites at some platform type of sites. Here the soils are deeply red from which red orhere may be obtained, while they are almost useless for cultivation. There are certain places among these where iron concentration is sufficient in the form of lateritic haematite to support some indigenous iron-smelting industry. In depression and on the lower flats, where drainage is checked and finer particles washed down also collect, the soils have darker hue, rainging between brownish and blackish, due to haematite and magnetite respectively. The occurrences of laterites used for indigenous iron smelting may be mentained at Nandinitola Akalberia and Rajdhar villages of Durg district and at some places in Raipur district upto 1970s. Here it is pertinent to point out that in this area limestone, bauxite, iron ore and coal were present which may be called the four pillars on which the modern industries of Chattishgarh developed. This area was not included in the Asur/Agaria/Munda belt of traditional iron smelters of India.

The Archaean rocks[10] of the area are known as Dharwarian" sediment which form a basement on which all younger sedimentary rockformations rest. They are generally highly metamorphosed[12] and unfossiliferous which suggests that there was no life on the earth at the time of their formation. As the structure and composition of the rocks are very complex they are often called "Fundamental gneiss" or "Basement Complex". The Dharwarian sediments contain largest iron ore deposit of the world in the form of haematite with Quartz[13] and Jasper[14]. It contain 60% to 69% iron. It is pertinent to point out here that maximum iron age Megalithic culture in India was reported where under the neath of earth crust Dharwarian semiments are present e.g. Tamilnadu, Karnataka, Andhra Pradesh, Ratnagiri Distt. of Maharashtra, Durg and Bastar area of Chhattisgarh and Southern Singhbhum in Jharkhand. The metallographic study of Rajghat iron implement in Varanasi district of Uttar Pradesh by Bharadwaj also conform that the source of their iron ore was from the area of Singhbhum. By the process of metamarphosis these Dharwarian sediments are evolved into patches of Quartz magnetite and haematite ore. In eastern ghat the metamorphic product of Dharwar sediment is called as Khondalite [16] the name given by British geologist T.W. Walkar in 1902 in honour of the hill man of Khondas. In the area of Bastar, Khondalite contain high alumina with iron ore $(Al^2O^3.Fe^2O^3.3H^2O)$ so by weathering on it Ferruginous Laterite and Aluminous Laterite are formed respectively. It contain 40% to 50% iron. These Quartz magnetite and haematite are converted into Laterite[17] in the soild profile of the area by weathering under high temperature, dense forestation and high rainfall during Pleistocene phase under alkaline climate. It is formed by the cappliary action in the Savana type of vegetation by which acidic water percolate underneath the soil to ferrogenous aluminous rocks from early Pleistocene to middle Pleistocene.

During British period ethenic people of the Bastar area use to take laterite as a source of iron by surface scrapping or by open pit mining like African countries. Here it is also important that Bailadila was included in Mallet list of 18 iron ores areas in 1890, which is at present contains 610 million tons of iron ore.

Before the discovery of coal in 18th century A.D. Charcoal was used as fuel energy in pre industrial metallurgical furnaces. Here it is noteable that the calorific value of coal and charcoal is 6500 and7500 K.cal. per Kg respectively. Therefore, the combustion energy level of both coal and charcoal is almost equal. Charcoal is obtained by dry distillation of wood (heating without the admission of air) in compartment Kilns or stalls. It contains 80% to 90% solid (nonvolatile) carbon, 10% to 18% volatile matter (including moisture) 0.6% to 1.2% ash and a negligible amount of sulphur. Charcoal is highly porores (upto 70%), it burns well and it shoot up the temperature of the blast, furnace upto 1300 C. The raw material for charcoal i.e. wood was profusely forthcoming in the area of Chhattishgarh and still it is available abundantly.

Analysis of the local lateretic material and slag :

Lateretic Ore	*Sample I*	*Sample II*
Fe_2O3	46.48%	45.38%
Al_2O_3	18.21%	22.14%
SiO_2	21.02%	4.04%
CaO	4.14%	2.26%
Moisture	1.00%	6.38%

Slag Analysis	*Sample I*	*Sample II*
Metallic Iron	8%	6.24%
Fe_20_3	14.46%	18.16%
FeO	22.56%	12.02%
$A1_20_3$	16.26%	12.28%
SiO_2	18.27%	16.34%

Here both, sample I and II in the case of Lateritic ore and slag is obtained from different locality of the same area at Leelar in Dhamtari District. So the geographical contextual area of the ore and slag is the same. Although the trace element is not obtained in the above analysis of ore and slag but the chemical percentage of alumina ($A1^2O^3$ oxide (SiO_2) in both the case of slag and ore compels to think that the megalithic people of the area obtained iron from the ore in the same vicinity.

In laterite, the Silica (SiO_2) and lime (CaO) is functing as flux[19] in the reduction of iron oxide into iron and also it lawering the melting point of the gangue (non metallic impurities of the ore) and removed it from the slag in smelting furnace. The melting point of the gangue is usually 1730^{0}C to 1990°C but when it in contact with flux, its melting point reduces to 450°C. So by the help of flux, non-metallic impurity of the metal is removed, much before it melted because its melting point is less then the melting point of the metal itself. So the presence of alumina in sample No. I (16-26%) and sample No. II (12 28%). and silica in sample No. I (18.26%) and sample No. II (16.38%) clearly indicates that flux was used by the local people in their smelting at Lillar. The Liller iron slag is primary in nature because it contains lime, silica, alumina and iron oxide. When this primary slag is again melted at 1160° to 1200°C then wrought iron is extracted and non metallic impurity removed but in wrought iron 1% to 3% iron silicate of slage is evenly distributed throughout the material in thread and fibrous by which it is very tough and rusting is very slow on it in contrast to cast and pig iron. The microwear study of wrought iron conform its fibrous nature and not crystalline like cast iron by which it can be easily shapable, while cast iron is very brittle. Although no study of iron object at Liller is done but the aforesaid analysis of slag conform its wrought iron character.

NOTES AND REFERENCES

1. The Lithosphere (Lithos = stone; sphere = round) is the outermost shell of the earth in solid state which is 10 km beneath of the sea level and 50 km

beneath the continents. It cover only 1% the radious of the earth while rest 99% of the earth in inner core in the form of liquid iron stage at temperature of 7000K" or 6727"C.

2. Copper Ore : Malachite ($CaCO_3.Cu(OH)_2$), Azurite ($2CuCO_3.Cu(OH)_2$), Cuprite (Cu_2O); iron ore : Haematite (Fe_2O_3), Magnetite (Fe_3O_4), Laterite ($Fe^2O^3.Al^2(OH)^4Si^2O^5$) Limonite ($2Fe_2O_3.3H_2O$) Siderite ($FeCO_3$).

3. Copper Ore : Chalcopyrite ($CuFeS_2$)

4. Pearson, G.; *Philosophical Transaction of the Royal Society of London* (London, 1795) pp. 322-323.

5. Furnance is a closed heating chamber which never to be opened, because the optimum temperature in open heat chamber is 800°C, while in closed heating chamber it exceeded from.800°C to 2000°C and so on. Blast means sudden throw of air to the furnance by mechanical process like bellow or blow pipe. So in blast furnace combustion of fuel in a closed chamber with high speed air increased the temperature as well as its reducing condition. Techenically blast furnance is a must for iron smelting, but not in copper or other metal smelting whose melting point is less then 800°C. In *Śatapatha Brāhmana* (i.i.2,7; 6,3,16), *Bhastrā* denotes a leathern bottle or pouch which used as air bellow in blast furnace. This textual confermation of blast furnace in Later Vedic text is also supported by the list of different metal given in *Vājasei Samhitā*. हिरण्य च येऽश्च यक श्यामं च ये लोहं च ये क्षीसं च ये त्रयु च ये पतेन कल्पन्ताम्। (18.13)

6. At a temperature of 1200° C, iron oxide could be reduced to the metallic and solid state, provided the partial pressure of oxygen was low and $CO:CO_2$ ratio in the carbothermic environment high. The temperature in the hottest part was around 1200°C and although reduction took place due to low pressure of oxygen and high ratio of $CO:CO_2$, the metallic product was not liquid but a spongy mass. The spongy mass was incorporated with slag, mostly fussible ferrous silicate or fayalite (melting point is 1170°C). The slag had to be squeezed out of the sponge iron by hammering at or above the temperature (1170° C)ṭa process known as forging. Hammering produced a continuous network of iron grains, sometimes interrupted by stringers of remaining slag elongated in the direction of the deformation of the iron bloom.

7. The Cuddaph has been named after the Cuddaph basin of Andhra Pradesh where it is best developed over the schists and gneisses of Archaean age and is overlain by the Vindhyans. It occupies an area of about 35000 square kilometers

and are 6 milometers in thickness which is mostly unfossiliferous. In India Cuddaph rock formations occur in Andhra Pradesh, Chattisgarh, Bijapur district of Karnataka and along Aravalli mountain in Rajasthan.

8. The Archaean system is made up of very ancient rocks such as gneisses, schists and granites and it forms a basement on which all younger sedimentary rock formations rest. The structure and composition of the rocks are very complex which covered at least two third portion of the Peninsular India and below the alluvium of the Ganga river between Bihar and Assam.

9. The Archaean rocks which are best developed in Dharwar region of Karnataka and the adjoining states. The sediments of the Dharwar supergroup were deposited over a basement of the Fundamental gneissic compelx. The rocks is of sedimentary origin with banded-haematite-quartzite, limestone, chlorite-schist, micaceous-quartzite and conglomerate.

10. The rocks of the Archaeozoic era were formed in the earlier part of Precambrian time.

11. It contain 20.000 million tone of iron ore.

12. Metamorphosis is the conversion of rock into earth crust under high pressure, high temperature and by the chemical action under material condition but not by weathering.

13. The quartz (SiO_2) is a colourless transparent, crystalline rock access in most ignores, metamorphic and sadimentary rocks. It is the commonest gangue mineral of ore deposits and forms the major portion of sands, and has wide spread distribution in the form of hexagonal crystals or in crystalline or cryptocrystalline masses. Its hardness on Mohs scale is 7.0. It is common in the Archaean and Dharwar systems.

14. Jasper is a dense, opaque to slightly translucent, red, crystalline quartz containing iron oxide as impurity.

15. Bhardwaj, H.C. *Aspects of Ancient Technology* (Delhi 1979) p. 154-156.

16. Khondalite is quartz haematite-magnetite-sillimanite-graphite scheist named after Khonds inhabitants of Orissa. They are well developed in Kerala and Sri Lanka.

17. Laterite is by origin a Greek word means brick red colour formed in the tropical region of south India and Africa. Ther term was firstly used by F.

Buchanan in 1807 in context to Malabar hill of Kerla (Buchanan, F. A *Journey from Madras* 3 vols., Landon, 1809), It is a sequi oxide of alumina and haemetite (Al_2O_3; here the red colour of it is due to haematite (Fe_2O^3); $Fe_2O_3.3H_2O$) and Grey colour is by alumina ($A1_2O3.3H^2O$). It contain usually 40 to 50% iron and its softness is due to its water contant ($3H_2O$). When water is removed it is as hard as brick and by this character its used for house constraction in south India. It is the most important raw material of indigenous furnance which produced pig iron during pre-industrial time in India.

18. Mallet, F.R., "Iron ore of India" in chapter IV of Watt, George, *A Dictionary of Economic Product of India* (London, 1890).

19. Flux is help in lowering the melting point of the non-metallic impurities of the ore from 1990°C to 600 C and removed it in the form of slag in iron smelting blast furnace. Here non-metallic impurities are in the form of silicate, sandstone with alumina, limestone, dolomite etc., whose melting point is atleast 35% greater than the melting point of iron. Flux is an additive assisting in fusion of non metallic material like $CaCO_3$, SiO_2 in metallic iron smelting, although the limestone also helps with slag formation. Here limestone is a rock of sedimentary origin containing the remains of marine organism or chemically precipitated or transported calcium carbonate. The pure mineral consists of $CaCO_3$ in the form of calcite, but rarely found commercial limestone contains iron oxide, alumina, magnesia, silica and sulphur with a CaO content of 22-56% and a MgO content of upto 21%.

Department of History, Culture and Archaeology
Dr. Ram Manohar Lohia Avadh University

5

PACHKHED NEWLY DISCOVERED MEGALITHIC HABITATIONAL SITE IN YEOTMAL DISTRICT, MAHARASHTRA

—Vilas Wahane

Earliest discovery of Megalithic burials in India was reported by Babington at Bangala Motta Parambri of Kerala in 1823 and initiated a new era in Indian archaeology.[1] Since then several megalithic sites were explored and some diggings were carried out in different parts of India (Mohanty and selvakumar 2002).[2] Just fifty years after the first finding, Rivett-Carnac (1869). Started the investigation in Vidarbha region, followed by many British Officials (Pears 1869, Carrey 1871).[3] However, problem oriented systematic exploration and excavation started only after independence. Agencies like the A.S.I., State Dept of Archaeology, Maharastra, Nagpur University and Deccan Collage Pune are engaged in research of this region. Interestingly from 18 th century onwards numerous sites were excavated in vidarbha region, hence a good data base is available. The study carried out oriented towards Distribution Pattern,[4] Socio-Economical Perspective,[5] Subsistence Pattern,[6] Trade and Exchange,[7] and Ethnoarchaeology (Gaitli Anuja 2004),[8] during Megalithic period in Vidarbha region. The typical features of Vidarbha Megalithic culture include the habitational sites and habitational-cum-burial sites which feature is rare in other parts of India. Earlier it was thought that megalithic people were nomadic and semi nomadic, but their monumental architecture and thick occupational deposits suggest that they had a settled economy and constructed their burials in a particular season of the year, may be after completion of harvesting. However, compared to the large number of burial sites, number of habitational sites is very negligible, the probable reason being lack of proper investigation and excavation around burial sites. The Megalithic people were the earliest iron using community in South India as well as in Vidarbha as is evident from the discovery of iron smelting furnaces, slags, ore and crucible fragments from the habitational sites like Naikund.[9] As against more than 3000 Megalithic burials located in about 100 sites, only twelve habitational sites have so far been reported from Vidarbha region. Of these, Takalghat-Khapa, Mahurjhari, Bhagimaheri, Khairwadi, Naikund, Pachkhedi, Bhavad and recently excavated habitational site Vyahad[10] are burial-cum-habitational sites- all situated in eastern Vidarbha, while the other four sites are habitational sites of which two are located in eastern Vidarbha like Paunar (Wardha district) and Adam (Nagpur district) and the other two—Kaundinypura (Amravati district) and Arni (Yavatmal district) are situated in western Vidarbha. Till now, Khairwada (Wardha district) is the only site which has yielded more than 1500 burials.

In this context, the recently discovered habitational site at Pachkhed in Yavatmal district assumes significance as it adds one more large site to the already known two megalithic habitational sites in the western region of Vidarbha.

Location and Geomorphology :

The megalithic habitational site at Pachkhed is located on the left bank of river Chandrabhaga and about 1 km south-east of the confluence of the two rivers, Chandrabhaga and Wardha. The village Pachkhed is under the jurisdiction of Babulgaon tehsil of Yavatmal District of Maharashtra. It is located 3 km east of village Shindhi on Pulgaon-Babulgaon road and 43 k.m away from Yavatmal town and about 70 km north of the famous megalithic habitational site at Arni excavted in early 1980s by the Department of Ancient Indian History, Culture and Archaeology, Nagpur University, Nagpur.[11] Thus, after a gap of nearly 25 years, a new megalithic habitational site has been discovered. This newly discovered habitational mound is locally known as *Sasu-suneche Ukande* {The Drum of Mother-in-law and Daughter in Law} The above two rivers must have played an important role in the sustenance of the site due to the availability of plenty of water, vegetation, wild animals and the aquatic animals coupled with the fertile soil of this region. At present, the ancient mound is divided into two smaller mounds (PKD-I and PKD-II), some 30 m apart, as a result of indiscriminate earth quarrying by the villagers in the recent past.The entire mound measurers about 250 x 70m with 6 meter thick occupational deposit.

PKD-I

This mound is sloping towards northern side and faces towards south where the section is visible. The mound measures 6 meters in height from the ground level. At the top of the mound there is a flood deposit of 5 feet. The section of this mound shows 10 habitational layers along with floor levels containing ash, charcoal, lime and burnt clay. Each habitational layer is about 10 cm thick.

PKD-II

This mound has a slope towards the southern side. The west facing section is close to the Pachkhed-Yeran road. The extant thickness of the mound is 5 meter. Like PKD-I here also one can notice the same flood deposit on the top. This deposit contains clay, sand and shells. At the base of the eroded flood deposit the remains of a soakage pit built of wedge-shaped bricks can be seen. The bricks measure 33x25x18 cm. The surface of the mound has yielded pestle and quern fragments of early historical period. The lower levels have yielded sherds of black-and- red ware, black ware and red ware, the shapes are vases, knobbed lids and bowls. The similarity in the make up and contents of the two mounds suggests that the two present mounds belonged to one big mound.

CERAMIC ASSEMBLAGES

(1) Black-and-red Ware

(2) Micaceous red Ware

(3) Black Ware

(4) Black slipped Ware

(5) Black painted micaceous red Ware

(6) Red slipped Ware

(7) Fine red slip Ware or Red polished Ware?

(8) Dull red Ware

(9) Terracotta tiles

The pottery types include Handis, vessels, bowls, basins, lipped vessels, lidded bowl, knobbed-lids and dishes. Black- and- red Ware and Black Ware are of medium fabric, while the Micacious red Ware includes both thick and medium fabrics. The Black slipped Ware is of very thin fabric.

So far as the other findings are concerned fragment of a bone point and one chalcedony blade is found. The black painted micaceous red ware found from this site is comparable with the pottery reported from the megalithic habitation-cum-burial site at Naikund.[12] All these potteries show that the site was first occupied by the Protohistoric people. The presence of red slipped ware, red polished ware?,wedge shaped bricks, pestles and querns show that the habitation continued up to the historical period. Similar type of soak-pits/ring wells built of wedge-shaped bricks have also been reported earlier from Arni and Adam in the Satavahana context.[13] The availability of bone point and one chalcedony blade from this site may indicate the presence of chalcolithic culture at this site. Similar type of bone- points and chalcedony blades have been reported from Tuljapur- garhi and Adam.[14]

Discussion :

The Pachkhed site seems to be an important link between the Megalithic cultures of Eastern Vidarbha and Western Vidarbha. From the western Vidarbha comprising of the districts Yavatmal, Amravati, Akola, Wasim and Buldhana, not a single megalithic burial is reported so far. The sites of Arni and Kaundinyapur have yielded only two sites each of the megalithic habitational site which were excavated. The present site will be second located in Yavatmal District and third one in the entire Western Vidarbha till date. Extensive and systematic exploration may yield some sites in this part of Vidarbha. The megalithic people seem to have inhabited here for a long time. As the site is being disturbed by villagers, it needs immediate protection and excavation.

The following questions arise after studying the environmental setting, nature of the site and the associated material culture:

1. Can the megalithic community of the Western Vidharbha have any affiliation with the eastern Vidarbha?
2. Or did they belong to two different cultural groups?
3. Does the size of the site and the greater thickness of the occupational deposit of Pachkhed site indicate that the western Vidarbha megalithic culture is earlier than the other sites of Eastern Vidarbha?

I believe that thorough explorations and systematic excavations of some potential sites from both these regions alone can answer these questions.

REFERENCES

(1)	Babington, J.	1823	*Description of the Pandu Koolies in Malbar,* TLSB, 3
(2)	Mohanti, R.K. Selvakumar, V.	2002 1997	*The Archaeology of Megaliths in India 1947—In Indian Archaeology in Retrospect* Vol. I, (Eds Setter and Ravi Korisetter)
(3)	Carrey, J.J.	1871	*Stone circle found Near Khariwada, Wardha District*, PASB.
(4)	Mohanty, R.K.	1993-94	*Vidarbha Megalithic: A New Perspective for Field Investigation,* Bharthi 20 Varanasi; Deo S.B. *Excavation at takalghat and khapa* (1968-69) Nagpur.
(5)	Deo, S.B. and K. Paddya	1985	*Recent Advances in Indian Archaeology* Deccan College Pune.
(6)	Thomas, P.K.	1993	*Faunal Remains from the Megalithic Habitation site at Bhagimohari, Maharashtra*, Man and Environment XXIV.
	Kajale, M.D.	1989	*Archaeological Investigations on Megalithic Bhagimohari and its significance for Ancient Indian Agricultural Systems*, Man and Environment XIII.
(7)	Mohanty, R.K.	1999	*Siginificance of bead manufacturing centre of Mahurihari, District Nagpur, Maharashtra, India*, in Man and Environment - XXIV(2).
(8)	Gitali, A.	2004	*A Living Megalithic Tradition of the Madia Gond of Gadchiroli District of Maharashtra*, Puratattva.
(9)	Deo, S.B. and Jamkhedkar, A.P.	1978-80	*Excavation at Naikund,* pp. 52-55.
(10)	Meshram, P.S. and Kellullu Ismail	(In press)	*Brief Report on the Excavation of Vyahad,* p.1.

(11) Indian Archaeology—A Review : 1978-79, *Excavation at Arni*, pp. 71-72. Ed. Thapar B.K.

(12) Deo, S.B. and Jamkhedkar, A.P., 1978-80, *Excavation at Naikund*, p. 20.

(13) Indian Archaeology—A Review : 1984-85, pp. 55, 56, ed. Tripathi, R.C. ; Nath, A. 1988-89, *Adam*, p. 119

(14) Bopardikar, B.P., Walimbe, Kajale, Thapar, B.K. 1984-85, *Excavation of Tuljapurgarhi*, p. 28 ; Nath, A., 1988-89, *Adam*, p. 89.

6

THREE NEW REVANTA IMAGES FROM BRAJ REGION

—*Vinay Kumar Gupta*

Revanta is one of the popular minor deities of the medieval period. His images were not properly identified till the beginning of 20th century as most of the scholars considered these horse riding figures as Kalki, the future incarnation of lord Viṣṇu or with the *Mahābhiniṣkramana* of Buddha. Pandit B.B. Bidyabinod first identified them properly in the collection of Indian museum, Calcutta quoting a verse from *Brhatsamhitā* (ch. 58, v. 56).

A number of literary works provide useful information about the birth of Revanta, his iconography and also the wide popularity of his worship in India. But an important aspect is that *Harivamśa Purāṇa* (ch. 9) and *Narasimha Purāṇa* (ch. 18), which give detailed description of Sūrya's family and his children, do not refer to Revanta, which indicates towards the lesser importance of Revanta during early centuries of Christian era.

In the *Viṣṇu Purāṇa*[1] (III, 2, 2-7), Parasara narrates to Maitreya the following story about the birth of Revanta. "Sanjñā, the daughter of Viswakarma, was the wife of the Sun God and gave birth to three of his children- Manu Vaivasvata, Yama and Yamuna river. Unable to endure the fervours of her lord, Sanjñā gave him Chhāyā as his handmaid and went of forest to do devout *tapas*. The Sun God, mistaking Chhāyā as his wife, begot three more children from Chhāyā-Śanaiśchara, Manu Savarṇī and river Tāpti. One day in some anguish Chhāyā denounced an imprecation upon Yama and hence revealed her identity as Chhāyā. After realising

---

* Research scholar, National Museum Institute, New Delhi.

the truth, Sun beheld Sanjna by the eye of meditation engaged in *tapas* in the form of a mare in the Uttara Kuril region. Sun himself took the form of a horse and rejoined his wife and begot three other children—the two Aswina Kumāras and Revanta, after that he brought her to his own dwelling.[2]

In the *Mārkaṇḍeya Purāṇa* Sūrya is said to have appointed Revanta to the lordship of Guhyakas and had told, "Thou shalt indeed be worthy of worship by the entire world, my child; and mortals who shall call thee to mind amid the terrors of forests and other lonely places, of great conflagrations, of enemies and robbers, shall be delivered out of great calamity. Comfort, intelligence, happiness, kingship, perfect health, fame, exalted position—these, when worshipped and well satisfied, thou shalt bestow on men.[3]

In the Prabhas Khanda of *Skanda Purāṇa*, Lord Śiva emphasizes the worship of Revanta and relates to Umā that after performing certain *pujā* etc., one must have a *darśan* of the Rājyabhattāraka Revanta seated on horse-back, as by doing so one will be free from all the evils and attain religious merit.[4]

The *Kalikā Purāṇa*[5] tells that "kings should worship Revanta at the gates according to the principles of sun worship. His image should be placed on a white horse with his hair fastened by a cloth. The deity should be dressed in a coat of mail and should carry a sword in his right hand and a whip in the left." The *Agni Purāṇa* calls him a horseman.

The earliest representation of Revanta in art is found in Gupta period, 5th -6th century A.D., in the form of images from Nagari (Chittor, Rajasthan), Newal (Unnao, U.P.), Jahangira hill (Bhagalpur, Bihar), Pachar (Gaya, Bihar) etc.[7] The important aspect about the find places of Revanta images is that these are generally found in northern India, in Gujrat, Rajasthan, Uttar Pradesh, Madhya Pradesh, Bihar, Haryana and later on occasionally from Bengal, Orissa and Tamilnadu. The find- places are more or less related with trader's activity, are those towns which acted as trade centres or were situated on various ancient trade routes.

After a detailed analysis we can say that the region of Mathura and Bharatpur districts, from where a number of Revanta images have been reported was an important centre of Revanta and Sun cult. The images of Revanta are represented in two styles, one in which only Revanta is shown riding a horse, holding the reins of horse in his left hand and a wine cup in the right hand, a sword or a dagger is shown tied to his waist. An attendant is shown holding a *chhatra* over his head and many other attendants accompany him in the hunting party. Here in this type of representation which appears to be quite popular in northern India, Dapda and

Piṅgala, two main attendants of Sūrya are not shown accompanying Revanta riding on their own horses.

The second type of images are those where these two attendants of Sūrya - Daṇḍa and Piṅgala are shown accompanying Revanta, one ahead of him and the other following him. This type of image appears to be the speciality of Mathura and Bharatpur region, from where no image of first type has come to light till now. Even when the images of second type are found outside this region, these are not far away from Mathura and are much later in date.

The three images being discussed here are the special products of Mathura and the nearby region. The first lmage (Pl. 1) has been found from a village named Harnaul of which actual name might be Haranpur or Huvishkpur, on the basis of linguistic studies. It is situated in the trans- Yamuna region of Mathura district near the famous site of Manth (Mat), near the ancient route going towards Ahichchhatra and other important places.

It is one of the early images of Revanta and probably the earliest of this type of imagery, belonging to late 6th century A.D. to early part of 7th century A.D. It is about 32 inches in height and is being worshipped as a female deity at a shrine near the huge mound, on which the village is situated. The sculpture is quite broken but some important information can be gathered from it.

The central deity is Revanta riding on a horse, holding reins of horse in the much broken left hand, while his right hand holds probably a wine cup. An attendant is holding *chhatra* over his head. Between the legs of the horses hounds are shown attacking the boars. One member Danda of the hunting party is completely missing while the figure of Piṅgala following Revanta is also much broken. The lack of sophistication of later Revanta images while narrating the whole hunting party episode and the stylistic features helps to ascribe it to circa 600 A.D.

The second image (Pl. 2) found during explorations is King at a shrine at the ancient mound of Aring (possibly ancient Aristapura). The ancient site of Aring is situated on the important trade route to Matsya and Mādhyamikā country. The town seems to be the ancient Saurapura which was on all accounts an important centre of Sun cult, which later came to be known as Ari.stapura. This image belongs to Pratihara period circa 10th century A.D. where all the sophistication in the representation of sculptural art is visible. The sculpture, which is about 30 inches in height is complete except for the faces which have been defaced by iconoclasts. In the top panel *Navagrahas* and *Astadikpalas* have been shown.

The central figure is of Revanta followed and preceded by Danda and Piṅgala. Lotus shaped parasols are shown hanging over all the three deities, held by Yaksas and Yaksis. Revanta is holding the reins of the horse in his right hand while in his left hand; he is holding a wine flask in which a female attendant is shown pouring wine. Gandharvas, the garland-bearers are shown flying near the parasols. Between the legs of horses, hounds are shown attacking the boars.

The third Revanta image (Pl. 3) found during explorations is from Mandoi mound, which is situated in front of another site Karhala in tehsil Chhata of Mathura district. The image is about 24 inches in height and is also being worshipped as some female deity as is the tradition in the whole Braj region. The sculpture belongs possibly to circa 9th century A.D. At the top panel *navagrahas* have been shown. The hunting party of the God is going in the left direction as is the case with the image from Harnaul. The other features include Danda following the deity and Piṅgala moving ahead of the deity. A person is shown holding a *chhatra* over the head of the deity. Danda and Piṅgala are shown without a *chhatra*. A *maladhāri* is shown standing in front of Piṅgala. A hound hunting a boar, this scene is possibly absent in this sculpture. It appears that a boar is shown under the feet of the horse of the main deity Revanta. Other details are not identifiable.

Two things are not clear at this stage—"why Revanta is shown holding a wine flask, while it is not mentioned in any ancient text" and "why hounds are always shown attacking the boars" because there are many more dangerous animals for a caravan or by that time had the boar become the only symbol of the evils?

Another important point that needs our attention is the fact that a number of horse rider types of terracottas have been reported from various north Indian medieval sites. Whether that was related to Revanta worship, is not clear yet. In the same way it came to notice that in several parts of Bihar, a number of people of lower social class offer clay horse rider figurines to a deity named Sahalag devata under a tree. Whether this local legend is inspired by the legend of Revanta who was actually born in some very out of order circumstances, also needs to be examined. Although Revanta cult was quite popular in Bihar as some of the early images found from this part of country indicate, whether in the later period the same major cult got transformed in a local tradition or not requires to be looked in.

Overall it can be said that Mathura and its adjoining part of Rajasthan formed an important centre of Revanta worship by its rulers and traders. Besides these three sculptures, four or five other Revanta images are already known from this region, all of which belong to Pratihāra period. But the Harnaul image adds a new dimension to it because of its late Gupta dating.

REFERENCES

1. *Viṣṇu Purāṇa, Tran.* Wilson, H.H., pp. 214-15.
2. Sharma, B.N. *Iconography of Revanta,* pp. 26-27.
3. *Mārkandeya Purāṇa,* Tran. Pargiter, F.E., CVIII, pp. 575-76
4. *Skanda Purāṇa,* Prabhasa Khanda, 164,1-4
5. *Kalikā Purāṇa,* 85, 46-49
6. For all the above references see Sharma, B.N., *op. cit.*
7. Sharma, B.N., *op. cit.*, p. 41.

7

GOLD COINS AT HAZARDUARI PALACE, MURSHIDABAD (W.B.)

—*Dr. G.S. Khwaja**

The Hazarduari (One Thousand Entrances) Palace at Murshidabad in West Bengal is one of the largest living places of India. A good specimen of Indo-European architecture with significant influence of Italian style, this palace was built by Nawwab Syed Mubarak Ali Khan, Humayun Jah (1824-38 A.D,) the Nawwab and the *Nazim* of Murshidabad State to hold *darbar* as well as provide lodging facility to British *sahabs* of East India Company on the bank of Bhagirathi. It now houses an archaeological museum of Archaeological Survey of India possessing some of the rare antiquities, paintings, arms and armours, manuscripts and coins. The collection reflects the taste of the Nawwabs who were connoisseurs of art.

Apart from many valuable antiquities this museum possesses, in its reserve collection, gold coins of different dynasties and rulers which, I feel, can be of great interest for numismatists and students of medieval history.

These gold pieces 18 in number represent Khalji Sultans of Delhi, Mughal Emperors, Nawwabs of Awadh *and* East India Company.

The Break-up of the coins as per the Dynasty King and metal is as follows:

GOLD COINS

KHALJI SULTANS OF DELHI

1. Alaud-Din Muhammad Shah Khalji____2 (Av. 1-2)
   (A.H. 695/1296 A.D.____A.H. 715/1316 A.D.)

MUGHAL EMPERORS

2. Jalalud-Din Akbar_____5 (Av. 3-7)
   (A.H. 963/1556 A.D._____A.H. 1014/1605 A.D.)
3. Shihabud-Din Shahjahan 1 (Av. 8)
   (A.H. 1037/1627 A.D._____A.H. 1068/1658 A.D.)
4. Muhammad Shah_____1 (Av. 9)
   (A.H. 1131/1719A.D._____A.H. 1161/1748 A.D.)
5. Alamgir II_____1 (Av. 10)
   (A.H. 1167/1754 A.D._____1173/1759 A.D.)
6. Shah Alam II_____1 (Av. 11)
   (A.H. 1173/1759 A.D._____1221/1806 A.D.)

NAWWABS OF AWADH

7. Nasirud-Din Haider Shah_____1 (Av. 12)
   (A.H. 1243/1827 A.D._____1253/1837 A.D.)
8. Muhammad Ali Shah_____1 (Av. 13)
   (A.H. 1253/1837 A.D._____1258/1842 A.D.)
9. Amjad Ali Shah_____1 (Av. 14)
   (A.H. 1258/1842 A.D._____1262/1847 A.D.)
10. Wajid Ali Ali Shah_____2 (Av. 15-16)
    (A.H. 1263/1847 A.D._____1272/1856 A.D.)

EAST INDIA COMPANY

11. Queen Victoria_____2 (Av. 17-18)

These coins are actually from the personal collection of Nawwabs of Murshidabad so has nothing to do with their circulation in that area or any other historical bearing for their being at Murshidabad.

Sl. No. Av. 1 and 2 are rounded gold pieces of Khalji Sultan of Delhi, Muhammad Shah entitled Alaud-Din (1296-1316 A.D.) and are of his *Sikandar-uth-Thani* type, minted at newly built city called Darul-Islam i.e. Siri, the Delhi City.

The obverse side contains the name of the Sultan whereas the reverse side bears the titles in a circle with date (in words) and mint-name in the margin. No. Av. 1 (2038) doesn't bear the date whereas No. Av. 2 (2040) a little larger in diameter is dated A.H. 713 =1313-14 A.D. The former too is datable between 1303 to 1314 A. D. on the basis of other finds of the same type.

The Arabic legends in Naskh characters are as under:

Obverse — *Reverse*

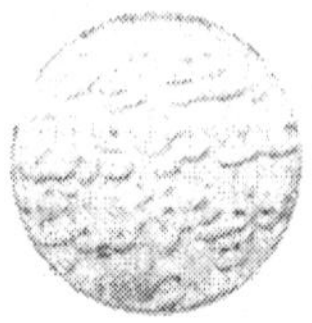

Obverse:

As-Sultan-al-A 'zam
Alaud-Dunya wad-Din
Abul-Muzaffar Muhammad Shah
As- Sualtan.

Reverse:

In the circle
Sikandar-uth-thani
Yamin-ul-Khilafat, Nasir-i-
Amirul-Muminin
In the margin
Duriba hadhal-sikka ba Darul-Islam
fi sana thalath ashr wa sitta mia.

Ref.: H. Nelson Wright—*The Coinage and Metrology of the Sultan of Delhi* (Delhi, 1936) p. 89, No. 305B.

Mughal Emperor Akbar (1556-1605 A.D.) is represented by five coins. No.Av.3 (2034) is a round gold piece of Emperor Akbar minted at *Darul-Khilafat*(i.e. Agra capital city*)* in A.H. 979=1571-72 A.D. The obverse side contains *Kalima* (First Creed of Islam) within the circle and names of Four Caliphs in the margin. The reverse side has the name of the Emperor, date and mint-name.

The Persian legends written in beautiful Thulth style are as under :

Obverse — *Reverse*

In the circle

Kalmia
Around
Ba sidq-i-Aba Bakr, ba adl-i-Umar,
Ba haya-i- 'Uthman, ba ilm-i-Ali.

Jalalud-Din Muhammad Akbar
Shah Ghazi khalladallahu
mulkahu ta 'ala (A.H.) 979
Darb-i-Darul Khilafat- Agra.

Ref.: Stanley Lane-Poole—*The Coins of the Moghul Emperors of Hindustan in the British Museum* (Landon,1892) P. 14, No.40, pl. II (date different)

No. Av. 4 to 7 are square gold issues of Emperor Akbar among them No. Av. 4 (2035) and Av. 5 (2036) are identical pieces. They are dated A.H. 988 = 1580-81 A.D. minted at Lahore. The obverse side of the coin bears the same religious text as that of the previous one (i.e. *Kalmia* and names of Four Caliph) but arrangement is different. The reverse side though contains the same legend as the earlier type but it is arranged in three horizontal lines in a square form.

The Persian legends in Nasta'liq characters are as under:

Obverse

Reverse

Ref.: Lane-Poole-*opcit.*, p.20, No.70, pl. III, V. P. Rode—*Catalogue of Coins in the Central Museum Nagpur,* Part I (Bombay, 1969) p.8, No. 45, pl. I.

No. AV. 6 (2037) is similar to No. Av. 4 but the date 987 = 1579 - 80 A.D. The name of mint on the reverse side is out of flan. No. A.v 7(2043) is again similar in words *(alaf)* alongwith the mint name *Urdu-i-Zafar Qarin* (i.e. the near - victory Royal Camp).

(Ref.: Lane-Poole - *op. cit.*, p. 20, No. 73, Pl. III)

Emperor Shahjahan (1627-58 A.D.) is represented by solitary coin No. Av. 8 (2046) which is a round gold piece dated A.H. 1043 = 1633-34 A.D., minted at Akbarabad (i.e. Agra), The obverse. side contains *Kalima* in a lozenge shape and names of Four Caliphs in the margin whereas the reverse side contains name of the Emperor and date, in figures, in the lozenge shape and titles and mint-name in the margin.

The Persian legends, written in beautiful Thulth characters, are as given below:

Obverse

Kalima
Around
*Basidq-i-Abi Bakr, ba- 'adl-i-
'Umar, ba-razm-i-'Uthaman-
o-ilm-i-'*

Reverse

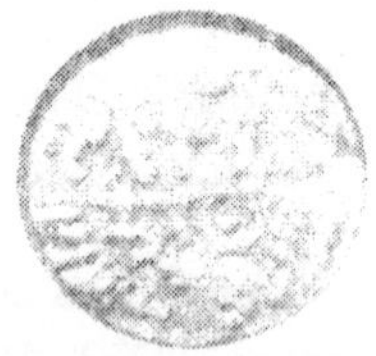

*Shihabud-Din Muhammad
Sahib Qiran-i-Thani, Shahjahan
Badshah Ghazi, 1043 Darb-i-
AlAkbarabad.*

Ref.: Lane-Poole - *op. cit.*, p. 110, No. 557, Pl. XV (but date different)

Among later-Mughal Emperors, Muhammad Shah (1719-1748 A.D.) is represented by one gold piece which is round in shape. Following the design of Emperor Aurangzeb's coinage this coin No. Av. 9 (2039) has text legends on both of obverse and reverse each divided into three horizontal lines. The coin is dated in 14th Regnal Year and A.H. 1144 =1731-32 A.D. (Unitary digit is cut off), minted at *Darul Khilafat* (Capital City) Shahjahanabad (i.e. Delhi). The obverse side contains name and title of the Emperor and Hijri date whereas reverse side contains mint name and regnal year as 14.

The Persian legends in Nasta'liq characters are as under :

Obverse

*Sikka-i-Mubarak-i-
Sahib Qiran-i-Thani
Muhammad Shah Badshah
-i-Ghazi-(A.H.) 114[4]*

Reverse

*Sana 14Julus-i-
Maimanat manus
Darb-i- Darul-Khilafat
Shahjahanabad*

Ref.: Lane-Poole - *op. cit.*, 200, No. 964-similar to No. 959 pl. XXV

No. Av. 10 (2041) is a round gold coin of another later Mughal Emperor, Alamgir II (1754-59 A.D. Interestingly the legends on obverse side are composed in a verse mentioning title and name of the Emperor Alamgir II. The reverse side has the conventional mint-name and regnal year 4 - (A.H. 1170) 1757-58 A.D.

The Persian legends in beautifully laid out five lines in Nasta'liq characters are as follow :

Obverse

Sikka zad bar haft kishwar
hamchu taban mihr-o-mah,
Shah Azizud-Din Alamgir
Thani Badshah.

Reverse

Sana 4 Julus-i-
maimanat manus
Darb-i- Darul-Khilafat
Shahjahanabad.

Ref.: Lane-Poole - *op. cit.*, p. 222, No. 1663

One more later-Mughal Emperor Shah Alam II (1759-1806 A.D.) is representation herewith his solitary gold piece of the *hami-i-din* type in round shape. It is again of the style in which the legends are composed in verse from. The obverse side of this coin No. Av. 11(2042) contains title and name of the Emperor in verse. Whereas the reverse side has the regnal year and mint-name Suba-i-Awadh (i.e Lucknow) with mint mark of fish. It is dated interestingly in the 26th year of the Emperor's reign with irregular Hijri date of (A.H.) 1229 = 1814 -15 A.D. It is because of the fact that this particular coin was issued as late as 1814 A.D. by the East India Company in the name of Shah Alam Ii though he was not in the throne (Shah Alam II died 1806 A.D.).

The Persian legends in Nasta'liq Characters are as under:

Obverse

Sikka zad bar haft
kishwar saya-i-fadl-i-Ilah,
Hami-i-Din-i-Muhammad
Shah-i-Alam Badshah-1229.

Reverse

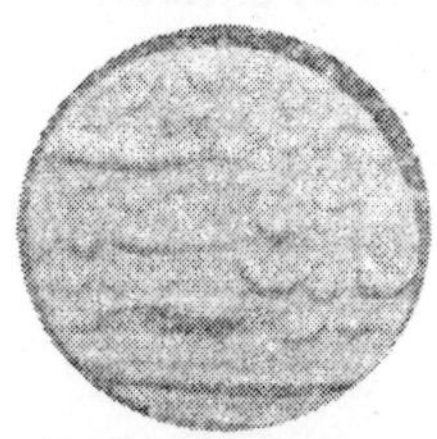

Sana 26 Julus
maimanat manus,
Darb-i- Suba-i-
Awadh (i.e. Lucknow).

Ref.: R.B. White head - *Catalogue of Coins in the Panjab Museum Lahore,* Vol. II (Oxford, 1914) p.378, No. 2859, Pl. XVIII.

Of these coins, five belong to a regional dynasty of Nawwabs of Awadh, who ruled from Lucknow. No. Av. 12 (2044) is a gold piece of Nawwab Nasirud-Din Haider (1827-37 A.D.) dated A.H. 1246 = 1830-31 A.D. On the obverse side it bears name of the Nawwab in the verse form with date in Hijri. On the reverse is imprinted the mint-name Lucknow alongwith the emblem of the state and regnal year 4.

The Persian legends in Nasta'liq characters are as under.

Obverse	*Reverse*

Sikka zad bar sim-o-zar azfadl-i-Haq zill-i-Rah, Naib-i- Mihdi Nasirud-Din Haider Badshah-1246.	*Sana 4 Julus-i- maimanat manus, Darb-i- Suba-i- Awadh (i.e. Lucknow).*

Ref.: John Allan - *op.cit.*, p. 35, similar to 57 a silver piece

No. Av. 13 (2048) is a gold issue of another Nawwab of Awadh named Muhammad 'Ali (1837-42 A.D.) minted at *Darus-Saltanat* (The capital city) Lucknow in the 2nd regnal year of the Nawwab and corresponding Hijri year 1254 = 1838-39 A.D. The obverse side carries the name and titles in verse and reverse side bears emblem of the state and mint-name around it with regnal year 2.

The Persian legends in delicate Nasta'liq characters are as under:

Obverse	*Reverse*
	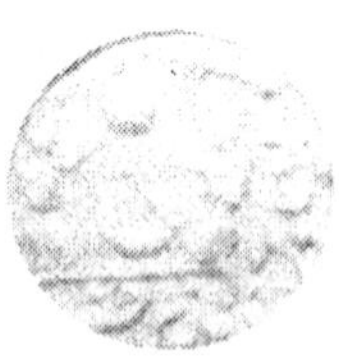
Bajud-o-karam sikka zad dar jahan, Muhammad'Ali Badshah -i-Jahan-1254.	*Sana 2 julus-i-maimanat manus. Darb-i-Darus-Saltanat Lucknow.*

Ref.: John Allan - *op.cit.*, similar to No. 112, p. 42 which is a silver piece)

No. Av. 14 (2045) is a gold coin of nawwab Amjad Ali (1842). This issue similar in design and layout to his predecessor is deted A.H. 1262 = 1848 A.D. in the 5th regnal year of the Nawwab from *Bait-us-Saltanat* (*i.e.* Abode of Sultanate or capital city) Lucknow.

The Persian legends in Nasta'liq characters are as follow:

Obverse

Darjahan zad sikka-i- Shahi
Ba taid-i-Ilah,
Zill-i-Haq Amjad 'Ali Shah-i-zamn
'Alam Panah - 1262.

Reverse

Sana 5 julus ṭi-
maimanat manus,
Darb-i-mulk-i-Awadh
Lucknow.

Ref.: John Allan - *op.cit.,* p. 45, No. 127 (a)

The last Nawwab of Awadh, Wajid 'Ali Shah (1847-1856 A.D.) is represented by 2 gold pieces round in shape and identical in legends, except dates. No. Av. 15 (2049) is the one issued in A.H. 1263 = 1846-47 A.D. and the 1st regnal year of the Nawwab from Lucknow mint. The obverse side contains name and titles in verse form. The mint-name and regnal year 1 alongwith emblem is on the reverse side.

The Persian legends in Nasta'liq characters are as below:

Obverse

Sikka zad bar sim-o-zar
az fadl-o-taid-i-Hah,
Zilla-i-Haq Wajid 'Ali Sultan-
-i- 'Alam Badshah - 1263.

Reverse

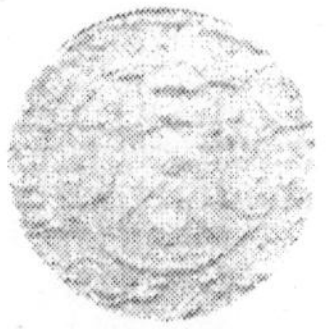

Sana Ahad julus-i-maimanat
manus, Darb-i-mulk-i-
Awadh, Baitus-Saltanat
Lucknow.

Ref.: John Allan - *op.cit.,* p. 49, No. 53 (a) Pl. II (6)

No. Av. 16 (2047) is another issue of the same type of gold coin of Nawwab

Wajid 'Ali Shah, issued in the next year of the previous issue. The date is A.H. 1264 = 1847-48 A.D. whereas the regnal year recorded is 2 of the Nawwab's reign.

No. Av. 17 (2032) and Av. 18 (2033) are two identical gold pieces of the same issue of Queen Victoria dated 1841 A.D. (probably minted at Calcutta). The obverse side carries the bust of the Queen, her name and date whereas the reverse side bears bilingual legends mentioning East India Company and denomination 'one mohur' in English and *'yak ashrafi'* in Persian inscribed around a lion under the coconut tree.

Obverse

Reverse

Ref.: Collin R. Bruce 1 *Standard Catalogue of World Coins* (Iola-WI, 1984, X Edn.) p. 980, No. 878-A4.1)

*Dr. G.S. Khwaja,
Deputy Superintending Epigraphist
(For Arabic and Persian Inscriptions)
Archaeological Survey of India
Old High Court Building, NAGPUR- 440 001
Phone: Off: +91712-2561955, Res: +910712-2593229,
E-mail: drgskhwaia@yahoo.co.in
Faizabad-224001

8

EXCAVATION AT SIRPUR, DISTRICT MAHASAMUND, CHHATTISGARH 2007-2008

—A.K. Sharma

In 2007-08 the author assisted by Prabhat Kumar Singh, Kumen Chandrakar, M.G. Goswami carried out excavations at Sirpur (21° 20'N, 82° ll'E) on behalf of Department of Culture and Archaeology, Government of Chhattisgarh.

To the north of priest's house there are three guest's rooms built abutting the outer face of the southern arm of the inner fortification wall. They all open towards the courtyard of the priest's house. Eastern one measures 4.45x1.40 m, middle one 2.50x1.40m and the western one measures 6.40x1.40m. The doors of the rooms are 0.80x0.80 m uniformally wide.

SRP-27

To the east of SRP-24, outside it's northern fortifications wall a Hari-Hara temple facing east has been unearthed. The twin *garbha-grihas* are built over a dressed Cuddapa stone *adhisthana* measuring 18.30x18.30x3.0 m. It is approached by 2.00x0.60 m steps numbering two. The five pillared covered *mandapa* is 11.25x7.0m and is approached by a 1.95x1.40x1.15 m gate which is topped by a well carved lintel stone which rests on stone brackets. *Antarala* is 1.40x0.95 m. Both the *garbha-grihas* are of same dimension i.e 2.0x2.0 m internally. The southern *garbha-griha* houses a white *Dhara-linga* whose height is 1.25 m and girth is 0.35 m. Height of the *yoni-peetha* is 0.38 m and girth is 0.45 m. northern *garbha-griha* houses a broken image of Vishnu represented only by it's lower part from the waist region and measures 0.60x0.58x0.29 m.

As the temple is located at a lower level than the Śiva temple complex no. SRP-24 and as it's sprawling stone paved courtyard on the eastern side is also at a

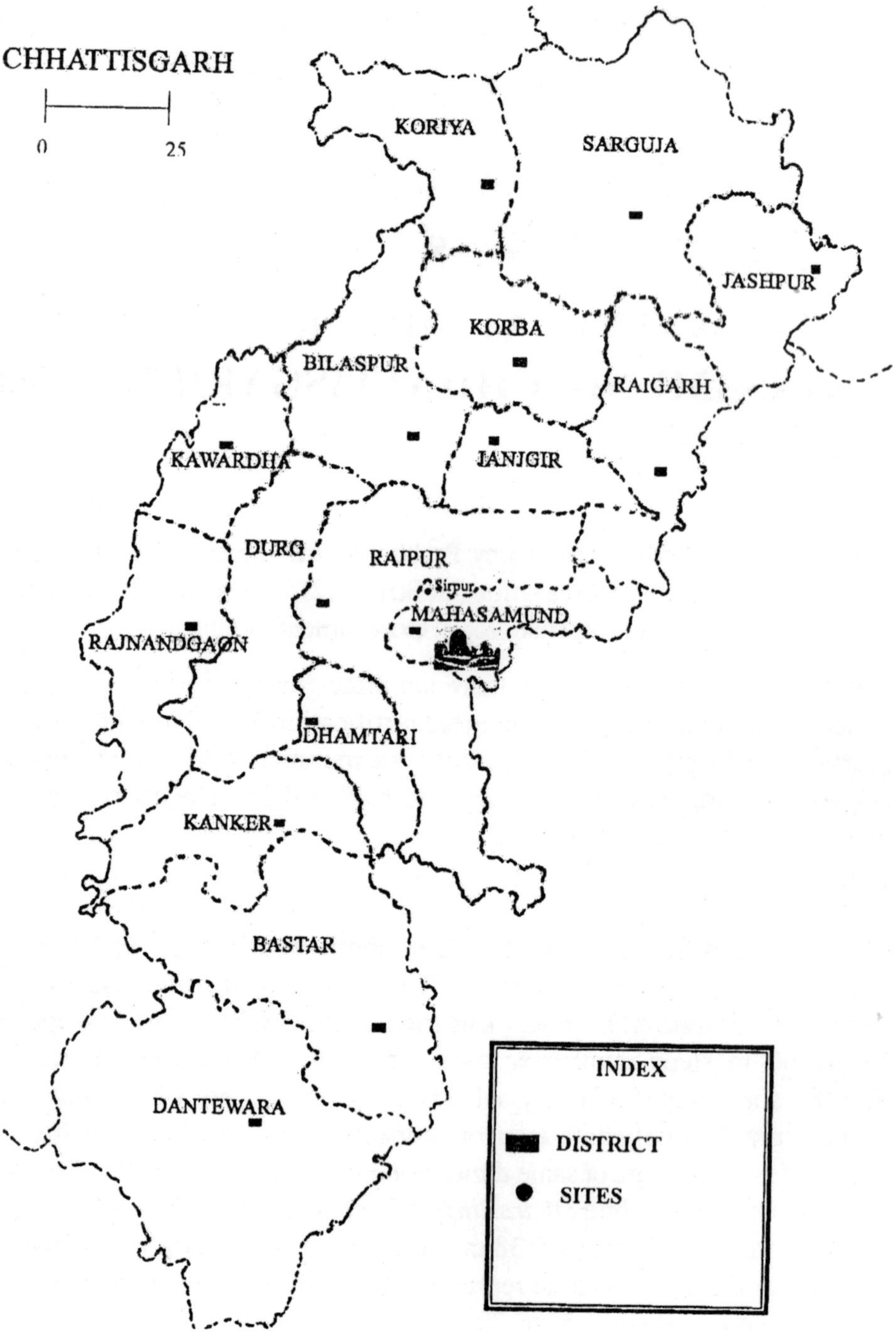

Fig. 8.1. Map of Chattisgarh.

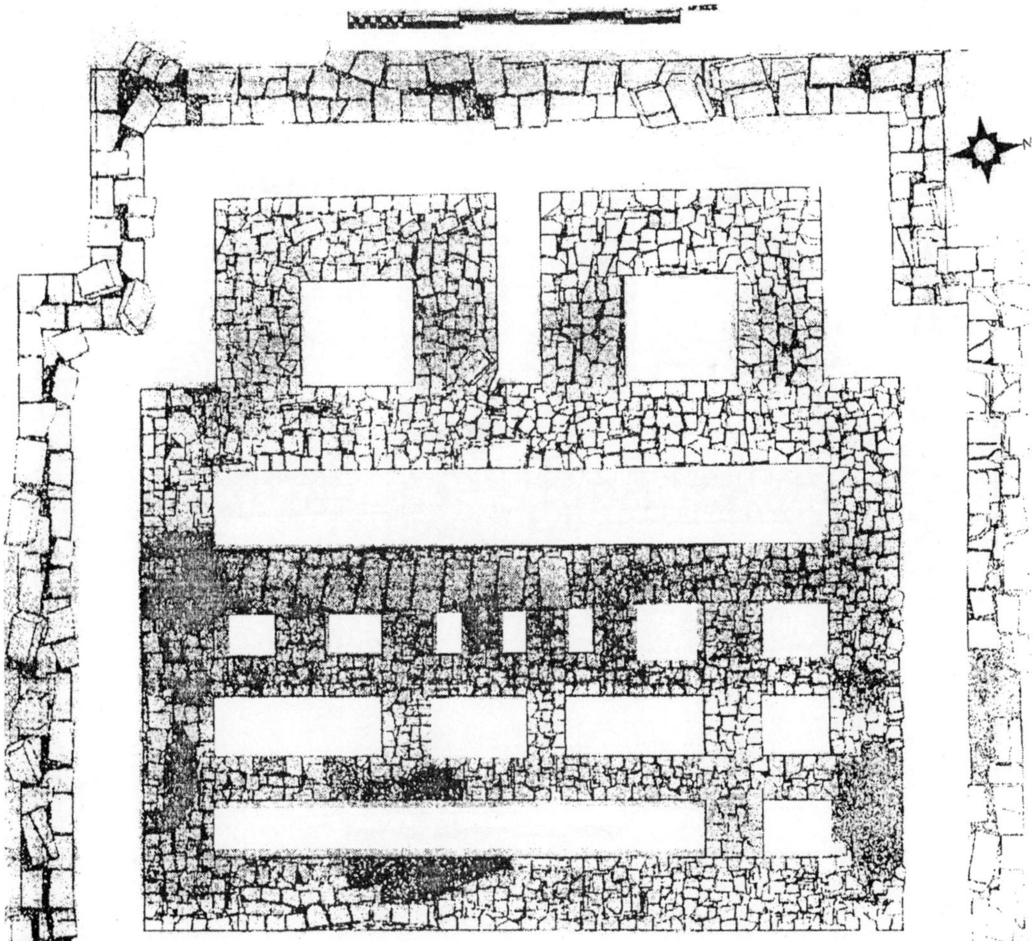

Fig. 8.2. Sirpur—Plan of SRP-27—Hari Hara Temple

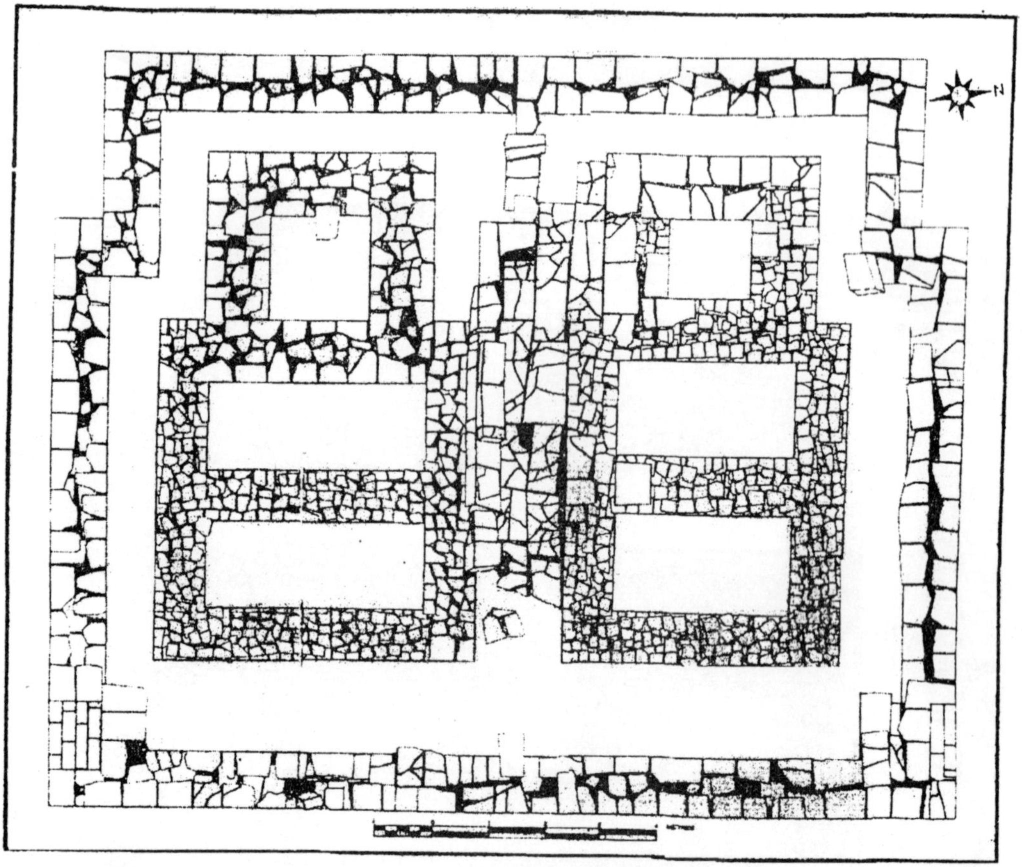

Fig. 8.3. Sirpur—Plan of SRP-34—Hari Hara Temple

lower level than that of SRP-24, this temple is earlier and was probably built during the fag end of Sarabhapuriya rule in Sirpur. Another evidence pointing to this aspect is that the covered drain of SRP-24 meant for draining out the water of the *garbha-griha* instead of following straight northern direction, flows obliquely towards north-east avoiding the Hari-Hara temple This indicates that Hari-Hara temple was already in existence when Somavanshis built the Śiva temple i.e. SRP-24

SRP-34

Another Hari-Hara temple with twin *garbha-griha* has been unearthed just to the east of priest's house . It is raised on a dressed stone platform *(Jagati)* having extent height of 1.25m, 13.40 m in length and 16.20m in width. It has two separate *mandapas* and *garbha-grihas* unlike SRP-27. The northern *garbha-griha* (1.40x1.40m internally) which houses a black granite, well polished Śiva linga measures 8.90x4.70 m externally. It has two pillared *mandapa* measuring 4.40x2.90 m having 1.20 x 0.90 m wide gate. The door of *garbha-griha* is 1.00 m wide.

The southern *garbha-griha* measures 8.90x5.20 m externally and has also two pillared *mandapa* measuring 3.80x3.50 m. The *mandapas* are covered by brick wall from sides, back and front. In all most all the temples and Buddha Viharas super structures were brick built. *Antarala* measures 1.20xl.0m . The front gates of *mandapas* are 1.20x0.90m wide, whereas the gate of *garbha-griha* is 1.0 m wide.

The platform *(Jagati)* is approached by two flight of steps located on the north-eastern and south-eastern corners. They have five steps each measuring 1.50x0.25x0.25 m each. The *sopanas* measure 1.50x1.0 m each. The walls of *garbha-griha* vary from 1.20 to 1.10 m in width whereas that of *mandapa* is 0.90 m.

Trideva Temple—SRP-33

To the farther east of SRP ţ 24, surrounded by paddy fields SRP-33 is located. It was found over grown with vegetation and much plundered for bricks and stone. The dig yielded a fortified Trideva temple facing west The fortification measures 30 m (north ţ south) x 34 m (east-west) and is entered through a 2.10 m wide gate, only the plinth stones of which are left. Near the entrance statue of Nandi carved out of red sand stone, measuring 0.75x.-35x.-50 m is located over which there is a four pillared *mandapa*. Just infront of Nandi in the centre of the space between the steps of adhisthana of *garbha-grihas* a *Sarvatobhadra* red sand stone pillar, with square cross section, depicting dancing Śiva on the eastern face, dancing Ganesh on the western face, Parvati on the northern face and Kartikeye on the southern face is placed.

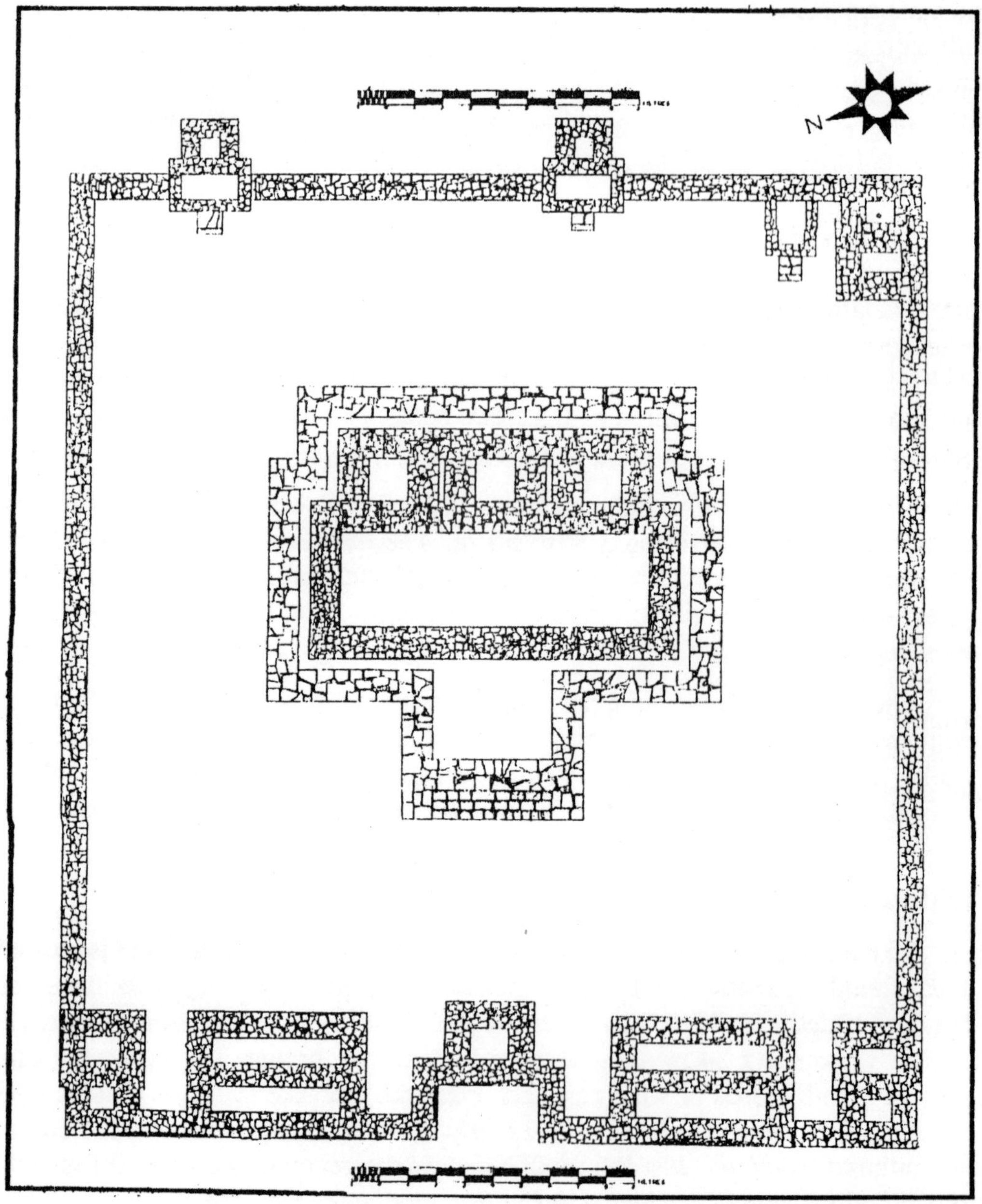

Fig. 8.4. Sirpur—Plan of SRP-33—Tridev Temple

The Tri-deva temple is raised on a 16.60 m (north-south) x 17.50 m (east-west) dressed stone adhisthana. It is approached be four flight of steps, 6.50 m wide and having arms as coping stones. The entire superstructure of the temple is brick-built with stone pillars, pilasters, brackets and carved lintels. The *mandapa* has two rows of five carved pillars and two plain pilasters. Each *garbha-griha* measures internally 1.50xl.50 m. In the central *garbha-griha* there is white *dhara* Siva *linga* measuring 0.95 m in height and 0.30 m in girth whereas *yonipeeth* is 0.56 m in girth. The water of the north ward pranala is cencealed below the floor of the adhisthana. The southern *garbha-griha* houses a broken image of Durga whose body below the waist region is present, in standing posture. Figure of lion is depicted below her feet. The third *garbha-griha,* the northern one probably housed an image of standing Vishnu, which was found in extremely broken and fragile condition.

The temple appears again to be a pancayatana type where as later on some more subsidiary shrines were added. On the east and west abutting the fortification wall four each have been unearthed, with only their foundation present but the recovery of two tiny figures of *nandi,* on speckled sand stone, directs towards at least two of them being Siva shrines.

Buddha Viharas

SRP-31—The badly plundred site to the north-west of Jaina- Vihara (SRP30), fortunately yielded few stone pillars and a hoard of bronze Buddhist statues numbering 79, few in good condition along with lumps of raw material, *gharia* with soot marks. These metal images comprise of 23 images of Buddha in *Bhumisparsa mudra,* 32 images of Bodhisattvas, one of Jambhala, five of Tara, five of Prajnaparamita, two of Vasudhara, one of Bhrikuti, one of Vajratara, eight stupa models, and one Vajra model. They measure in size from 18.5x8.00 cm to 7.0x4.5 cm.

They are masterly carved and few of them are silver gilted. Discovery of such a large hoard along with raw material and modeling instruments show that Sirpur had its own metal carving industry during th -8th century A.D. not much influenced by east or west. The statues prepared at Sirpur were traded to other parts of the country.

Attached below the pedestal of some sculptures 12 circular terra-cotta tablets inscribed with Buddhist Beeja-mantra were recovered.

SRP-32

Another Buddha Vihar, designated as SRP-32, located nearly 200 m to the north of Trideva temple (SRP-33) was unearthed. Due to extensive agricultural and brick kiln operations, hardly any structural remains are left except the rubble laid foundation of *mandapa.* The Vihara facing west had three *garbha-grihas.* The deities adoring the *garbha-grihas* could be partly recovered in extremely broken condition expect the main deity *i.e.* red sand stone Bhuddha in bhumi-sparsh mudra which was recovered at the depth of 1.80 m near the north-east comer of the northern *garbha-griha.* This Buddha is the finest so far unearthern at Sirpur. Two Bodhisatva images that might have been in the two side *garbha-grihas* were recovered only in fragmentary condition. The stone lion throne of Buddha was found intact.

From the constructional details it is apparent that at least the *garbhagrihas* were constructed reusing the stone structural remains of some temple. Fragments of lintel stone and pillars along with highly eroded sculptures were also recovered. Quantity of burnt bricks recovered show that the super structure was brick built. While the *mandapas* had stone pillars. *garbhagrihas* and *mandapa* were stone floored.

Jain Vihara

To the south of the main Śiva temple, residential quarters comprising of several rooms, bath-rooms, kitchen etc. have been exposed. Three clear floor levels, superimposition of walls and different constructional patterns along with pottery and antiquities recovered from this area indicate the presence of three structural periods i.e. *Sarabhapuriya, Somavamshi* and *kalachuri.*

During second period of occupation, probably, when the main Śiva temple was not much in worship, by modifying the rooms a Jain Vihara facing north was built. It comprises of a central pillared *mandapa* measuring 16.0x15.0 m, side walls of which are capped by huge rectangular laterite blocks. For draining out water from the open *mandapa,* a covered drain has been provided on the north-western corner. The fact that this drain passed through the rooms on western side indicates that it was constructed after the rooms of the period I fell into disuse. These rooms are brick constructions whereas later ones are stone constructions.

The rooms in front of *Mandapa* in north and south measure 3.90x2.30 m while those on the eastern and western side measure 4.90x2.50 m. The rooms adjoining north-south rooms measure 2.30x2.60 m. The *Vihara* is approached from north through a pillared entrance leading to a verandah measuring 11.10x2.10 m. From the *Vihara* four fragmentary stone sculptures have been recovered. Out of these two are heads with distinct three tier canopy and elongated ears while the other two are torso portions with thin waist typical of Jaina figures.

Antiquities

Apart from those mentioned above, a large number of Ganesha mini sculptures were recovered from the temple sites. Others include Ambika, Gouri, Surya, Vishnu, Vinadhara Siva and votive Siva lingas as well as Ayagpatta. Bronze objects include apart from images, as mentioned earlier, bangles, cutter, key ring. Copper pots, finger rings, hair pin, bangles along with ingots were also found. Beads made on semi-precious stone, bone, glass and terracotta also form part of the assemblage. Stone and terracotta dabbers, polishers, skin rubblers, gamesman were found in good quantity.

Amongst the house hold goods stone pestles, grinders, mulers, pounders etc. have been recovered in large quantity and in various shapes and sizes. The grinders particularly are of two types :

1. with vertical holds in the centre, met in case of larger and heavier ones are meant for grounding flour while.
2. The smaller and lighter ones with side holds for handles are meant for pulses as is the practice in Chhattisgarh villages even to this day.

In the *prangana* (courtyard) of priests houses, religious complexes and in one or two room and each house stone *(Okhli)* with round tapering holes were found embedded. They served for dehusking of cereal grains and paddy. Each unit appears to be self sufficient in this regard. Stacks of lime were also recovered to be used for white washing the lime plastered buildings during festive and ceremonial occasions.

Amongst the iron objects nails of various types and sizes including headless ones, arrow heads, sickles, chisels, door clamps, rings, dowels, hooks, knives, needles, pick-axes, plates, screw locks, spear head, sword blades, ladles etc have been recovered in large numbers along with raw material and waste. This shows that iron was being smelted in large quantity for supply to other places.

Town Planning

The area east and SRP - 34 and outer fortification wall of SRP -24 has been excavated to the length of nearly 70 m. east-west and width of 40 m. north-south. It has brought out the plan of a systematically laid town ship wide streets, row of houses, courtyards, performance platform and a stone lined well for fresh and clean water during rainy season.

The main street which runs north-south is first 6.10 m wide and then widens to 9.70 m. before approaching the main gate of Śiva temple (SRP-24). Probably it continued up to the river front which in hardly 100 m from the temple site. To the west of the street from north, there is a block comprising of eight rooms and three verandahs, two in the front and one on the north. The size of the two row of rooms varies from 2.30 x 2.00 m. to 2.10x2.25 m. The front verandahs are 5.20 x 1.20 m in size and have open front. Rooms are inter connected by 0.80 x 0.60 m wide doors. To the north of the verandahs an extra room limit of burnt bricks was added subsequently and measures 1.20x1.80 m. The two verandahs and the lioncel room are interconnected through ride doors.

To the south of this block along the street there is another block consisting of sixteen rooms in two rows of right room each. They are of the rise of 2.0 x 2.0 m., Parallel to the street in front of the front row of room they are eight shops, each measuring 2.25 x 1.50 m. They ware constructed by encroaching the street by 1.90 m. The shops are partitioned by a single row of bricks land on headers in order to same space. Each shop is connected with a back room of 2.0 x 2.0 m size to be approached by 0.80 x 0.60 m wide door having single fly door as the single door socket indicates. These room further open in another back room of same size. There room reserved as godowns. Room belonging to each shop are not connected with room of other shops. Shop fronts have larger blocks of shared saving as platform for display of goods and have 0.05 x 0.05 m square sockets at both ends for holding wooden posts. On the eastern ride of the street so for 18 room and two large verandahs there are no shops. To the back of these room there is another set of seven room and three large verandahs. Further to the east of there rows, newly 30 ms away another row of house have been unearthed along with a stone lined well with platform paved with lateritic blocks.

All the room and verandahs are stone floored except are which is brick floored. The eastern side blocks have in built grinders pastels and ponder sockets *(Okhli)* and are also provided with, water drains generally made of lateritic or lime stone blocks. The drains slope towards north-west ie. towards the river, in which direction the land slopes. All the residences are built up of biscuit sized lime stone pieces.

To the south of the eastern row of houses there is dressed stone platform measuring 7.70 m east-west and 10.30 m north-south facing west and approached by three flight of steps which served as performance platform on special occasion.

Muslim Period Silver Coins

From the upper layer of the excavations mostly form layer 1 and 2 silver coins belonging to sixth and thirty three regnal year of Shahjahan, minted at Surat and

Patna and that of Aurangzeb pertaining to his twelth regnal year and minted at Surat were recovered. One of his coins hears the legend Bundar-e-Mubarak Surat. Apart from these coins a terra-cotta seal with Persian legends belonging to Mughal Period, having impression of Aurargzeb's coin was also recovered. These recoveries from Sirpur shows that, unlike previous assumption, Sirpur remained alive not only as a religious centre but also as a thriving trade centre at least up to the period of Aurangzeb (1658-1707 A.D.)

The above mentioned coins, round in shape and some having punch holes are examples of adopting tradition of verses in the legends laid by the Gujrat Sultans. In these the metric Persian legends are beautifully written in nastaliq style in three bands. These coins were studied by Dr. G.S. Khwaja.

Pottery

From the lower levels datable to 5th-6th century A.D. pottery assemblage consists of Red Polished Ware having spouted vessels, bowls and basins in large numbers. Somvanshi level pottery datable to 7-9 century A.D. comprises of Black Polished ware, dull Red ware and Grey Ware. The shapes are mostly bowls, basin, lota, handis, dishes and storage jars. Large storage Jars *(Nands)* are generally made of thick coarse Red Ware. Generally black vessels ware used for either cooking purposes or for keeping pickles as being less pours they absorb less water and oil.

In all the levels, particularly from and around religious structures large number of earthen lamps and miniature offering pots were recovered. Along with them on particular religions occasion terracotta human and animal figurines are also offered which have been recovered in good numbers.

9

RECENT DISCOVERY OF ARCHAEOLOGICAL SITE IN BHABHUA (KAIMUR DIST.) BIHAR

—*Sachin Kumar Tiwari**

INTRODUCTION :

Kaimur District (24'25^0 N lat. 83' 40^0 E long.) is situated in South western part of Bihar Earlier it was known as Shahabad, Rohtas and Bhabhua. This place has been inhabited from prehistoric times on wards.[1] Geographically kaimur district is situated in the Ganga Son divide and hence it is fertile region. Kaimur region can be divided into three parts:

(1) Hilly region (2) Valley region (3) Plain region.[2]

All the rivers and it tributaries in this region flow through the kaimur ranges and some are perineal and some depend on monsoon rainfall. The rivers of this region Karmnasa and Durgawati river flow on its western side. Kudra river such as Dhoba, Kuhira river flows toward north where they meet the river Karmanasha which is interturn a tributary of river Ganga. This rivers not only make the region fertile but also acts us a natural fortification. Towards the south of the Kaimur region the hills provide natural barrier.

Archaeological activity of this region started from prehistoric times. When man habitated the hills and Valleys of Kaimur. However the plains were inhabited from c. 400 B.C. onwards till c. 1200-1400 A.D. (Kaimur Archaeological District Gazetter 2001, According to Pottery analysis).

During the ancient times Kaimur region was known by known by the name of KARUSH and it was the part of Magadh Empire, later this region came under the

---

* Institute of Archaeology, Red Fort, Delhi.

rule of Guptas and later Guptas and during the 700 A.D. it formed a part of *Harshavardhan's* empire. An inscription found from the Gupta Period temple called Mundeshwary situated in the Bhabhua region of kaimur district, rulers to a king having the little *Mahasamant Maharaj Udayasen* who ruled this region.[3]

Legend on the coins of Bengal ruler *Shashank* refers to place called *Rohtasgarh*. Which is identified with the modern region Rohtas situated west of Bhabhua. At one point of time Bhabhua was also a part of Rohtas district. *Si-u-ki* tells that *Huen-tang* travelled through the country in 7th cen. A. D. and passed through *Arrah* which was a part of shahabad region.[4]

This region was also rulled by the *Shail Dynasty* during 1200 A. D. (C. Mark). For the 1st time the entire kaimur region came under the rule of *Pala Dynasty.* This is known from *Tarachandi inscription* found from Sasaram (Rohtas District). After 1200 A. D. This region came under the rule of several rules like *Ujjain Rajput* and *Malwa Rulers* In 1193 A. D. When *Bakhtiyar Khilji* invaded Bihar, he defeated Rajput who where then the rulers of Shahabad region. After this defeat Bakhtiyar khilji ruled over Bihar and him Muslim rule started.[5]

LOCATION : The present area of study is situated in the northern part of Bhabhua block in (03^0 36' 25'' E.W. long. 25^0 2' 46'' N.S. latt.) Kaimur district. The nearest railway station is known by the name of Bhabhua road which is situated in the Mohania block (Kaimur district). The site is situated approx. 20 km. south of Bhabhua railway station, and is approachable by road.

PREVIOUS WORK : The entire Kaimur region is archaeologically rich and similar to other region this sites are situated either on the bank of the rivers or in the confluence of the rivers. Some are situated near the four hills also the natural and geographical position of these sites provides natural protection though the region was archaeologically rich not much has been done. Initially the region was surveyed by *BUCNON* and *GAIRIK*, but the results are not much complete, Between 1994-95 Dr. Prakash Chandra Prasad. State Dept. of Archaeology. Bihar has explored this district and discovered 66 sites spreading over to block of this district. This discovery serve as an example in the field of archaeological importance of this region. Out of this sites from Bhabhua block the team has explored 11 sites only. Further exploration can reveal few more archaeologically important sites as well.[6]

Team has bound pottery in the form of Red ware, Black ware, black and Red ware and form the temple are they had bound sculpture remains identified as Ganesha, Hanumana, Krishna avatara, Chaturmukhilinga, Umamaheshwar, Mahishasurmardini etc.[7]

RECENT EXPLORATION OF BHABHUA BLOCK : Drawing March 2008 the survey carried out by the scholar in Bhabhua block revealed few more sites which due to some reason could not be identified by the exploration team during 1994-95 exploration team reported site by the name Kudasan 6 km. N. W. of Bhabhua, however team could not explore beyond kudasan due to lack of inaccessible roads they explored the two routs from this sites one going east wards and other passing throw the middle of this village.

Present area of study in done on this area left by the explored team in 1994-95 that is of Mahasuan village. Jamuanva, Manihari, Kamharidevi, Rampur, Ruppur.

JAMUANVA : In this village fore mound are identified of these mound I & II are situated towards the Southern part of village. Mound III in western part of the village is still under habitation and has a government school. About 1 km. west of this site flows a river called KUHIRA toward Northern direction. Where it joint is to a Note which is about 100 m. west of mound II, but now they nala is water only seasonally.

Mound I is 310 in diameter and approx. 12 m. in height. On this a temple know by the name of *Jauhari Maa* is constructed. Mound II is 230 in diameter and approx 15 m. in height on this mound is situated an ancient shiva temple and near it there are abundant structures belonging to saints. It appears that the temple had successive additions in the post. Mound III is 300 in diameter and approx 12 m. in height. At present the entire village resets on the mound. Mound IV is of 200 in diameter and approx 4 metres in height.

From the study of the remains found from mound I, II & III it can be said that they are all part of a single settlement the distance between these mounds in about 3-4 m. From the study of the pottery type the age of the settlement is assumed to be stretching from (300 B.C. to 1200 A. D.

Sculptural remains were found all over the area mostly on mound I & II Umamaheshwar Sculpture was found in 3 fragment. One pannel depiction all the Avātāra of the Vishnu, Agnidev, Ganesha, Gandharva, Mahishasurmardini were also found. One broken head portion of and image appears to be of Buddha. The sculpture remains were found either completely exposed or partialy buried under the soil.

The details of antiquities fond are :

NO.	SCULPTURE & ANTIQUITY	DIMENSION IN C.M.	PLATE NO.	
1.	Umamaheshwar (2)	53x51x19		Fragmented, mad from Black Basalt Rock, Probably from Gaya and Rajmahal, Bihar.
2.	Uma Maheshwar (1)	43x37x16		-do-
3.	Mahishasur Mardni	62x35x14		Buff sand stone, Probably Kaimur hills, Bihar.
4.	Female Figurine	7x4x2.5		Fragmental made of T. C. light Bull in colour.
5.	Others			(i) Areccanut T. C. Blad (ii) Green colour grounded stone.

* Single moulded, Hair style is at Trefoil style and parting of the hair is decorated with Māngaticā middle of the head portion passing from the back is Judā. Just like figuring found from Ahichhatra. (Ancient India No. 4, 1948, pp. 104-105)

Similar many other stone images of various gods and goddess has been found in fragments. They measure approximately between 89x18x18c. m. to 14x10x5 c.m. Stylistically and iconographically these sculpture remains can be attributed to *Pala Period.* This is also confirmed by the available pottery remains and literary sources referring this region to be under Pala dominious. Some important pottery available from this site are as following:

(i) Bowl with vertical featureless rim and incurved side with a medium not to line fabric grey can and its polished internally the upper part of the external surface is polished bright black white the lower has a golden hill.

(ii) Dish with an interted externally grooved rim and incurved sided off medium fabric. It shows and black patches on the exterior surface.[8] etc.

MANIHARI : This village is situated 19 km. north of Bhabhua block, the scholar has identified a mound of village 200 in diameter and 18 m. in height. In this mound is highly disturbed due to modern human activities.

The pottery found from this site is as following :

(i) Miniature vase of R. W. having splayed out rim cancave neck globular body with a round base. It is of medium fabric having dull red core

(ii) Red slip sherds with an applique chord showing finger nail incisions.

(iii) Red ware vase with a splayed out featureless rim with grooved profile and a flattered body with lower girth of medium fabric it is treated with a crimson slip etc.9

KAMHARI DIH : Towards the west of the village manihari is situated Kamharidih which is about 450 m. from the village proper. Both the villages Manihari and Kamharidih are surrounded by rivers like. Durgawati in the north. Suara in the east, Kuhira in the west, all the three rivers flow towards the North and are situated 800 m. away from the village. Mound at kamhari dih is encroached by a government school.

This mound is about 500 in diameters and 2 m. in height. Form this mound a number of pot sherds and bangle pieces have been found. The people refer to this place as a bangle manufacturing area. The pottery found from this site is as following:

(i) Red ware vase with an out twined featureless him and a concave neck.

(ii) Lid of dull Rid ware with thickened undercut rim base and a flat terminal of medium fabric it si devoid of any slip or vase.[10]

RAMPUR : The village is situated 10 km. North of Bhabhua block, towards the South west of this village a mound 500 in diameter and 5 m. in height. Around this mound agricultural activities are going on and hence the size of the mound is gradually deareasing. Towards the west of this village flows the river SUVARA. Both the rivers are at the distance of 700 m. from the village pottery type are same.

RUPPUR : Towards the west of Rampur is situated another village called ruppur with the river Durgawati flowing towards its north. A temple situated in this village with an ancient idol in its sanctum but it difficult to identified the image as it has been smeared with the sandal paste.

SCOPE OF THE WORK :

Aim of this present is to bring the archaeological fruit or wealth as importance of this regions in front of scholars. It is also the view of that much more work has to be done in this region so that more work has to be done in this region so that many more archaeological sides could be brought to light which are under the threat of destruction due to passage of time. There sites are rich in sculptural wealth and which needs. Protection from further distraction. It is unfortunate that not much work has been done in this region. Both in the hilly region and plains. It can be said that further work is this region may fill many gaps in the chronological frame work of this region.

DISCUSSION :

This region is naturally well protected by the Kaimru range on one side and the river and its tributaries on the other side. Some of the mounds in this region measures 10.11 m. in height and have a diameter of 400 m. So from the thick deposit of these Mounds it can be said that this was a highly populated area in the past.

The places like Jamuanva from where a number of sculptural fragments were found shows that this place might be an important religious place with a huge temple complex. These sculpture where made of Black and Brown colour Basalt rock the source of which can be from Gaya and Rajmahal hills. It is possible that either sculpture were manufactured in that region or raw material was brought from that region. In either case it shows the connection between these two regions during Pala Dynasty.

This region gets its importance from the fact that it lies in the middle of the ancient trade route. Kannauj which is situated to the north west of this region leads to Varanasi and from there to Pataliputra and Gaya.

The T.C. figurine found from the eroded portion of Jamuanva Mound No. II shows similarity with the T.C. female figurine found from Achichhatra in its hairstyle dress and ornamentation. This again shows some connection between these two regions, especially in the field of art.

From the study of the potsherds collected from the surface of the mound of Jamu anva it can be said that the site was inhabited from *c*. 400 B.C. onwards.

The site discovered during the survey of 1994-95 are situated 2-4 km. away from the present sites discovered in march 2007. The region is thickly populated and well developed. The graphical conditions of this region must have also played an important role in the prosperity of this region.

ACKNOWLEDGMENT : I am greatly thankful to Dr. B. R. Mani, Dr. R.

N. Singh, I. M. Tikoo, Vishnu Kant Sharma, Dr. Sarjun Prasad, Ankhit Pradhan for there valuable suggestions and guidance.

I am also thankful to my brother Amitabh Tiwary, friends Virag Sontake, Krishnamurti, Prachi and my colleagues who helped me in many ways.

REFERENCES

1. Kumar Anand, Early Medieval Sculpture Art of Kaimur. 1993-94 *Journal of Bihar Puravid Parisad*, Vol. XVII & XVIII (Jan.-Dec.) (Ed. Dr. Bhagwat Sahal), Patna, p. 204

2. Sinha, A. K., 2001, *Kaimur Archaeological District Gazetteer,* Directorate of Archaeology Dept. of Art & Culture and Youth, Government of Bihar, Patna, p. 4

3. Krishna Deva, 1996, *Temples of India*, Vol. I, Aryan Books International, New Delhi, pp. 32-33

4. http:// www.mapsofiindia.com/maps/bihar/districts/bhabhua JP9 4.26.08

5. Ibid

6. Sinha, A. K., 2001, *Kaimur Archaeological District Gazetteer*, Directorate of Archeology. Dept. of Art & culture, government of Bihar, Patna, p. 4

7. Ibid., p. 5

8. Sharma, G. R. 1949-50. *Excavation at Kausambi*, memoirs of the A. S. I. No. 74. New Delhi, pp. 136-140

9. Ibid., pp. 148-150

10. *Ancient India*, No. 10811 (954-55). Bulletin of the A. S. I., pp. 27-81

11. Sharma. R. C. 1991, *The Pala Idiom of sculpture Art in studies in Archaeology.* (Ed. Asok Datta) Books & Books, New Delhi, pp. 209-215

12. Kumar, Anand, 1993-94. Early Medieval Sculpture Art of Kaimur *Journal of Bihar Puravid Parisad*, Vol. XVII & XVIII (Jan.-Dec.) (Ed. Dr. Bhagwat Sahal), Patna, pp. 206-207

13. Agrawal,V. S., 1948, *Ancient India*, No. 4, pp. 104-105.

10

ARCHAEOLOGICAL REMAINS OF CHOUDWAR, DISTRICT CUTTACK, ORISSA

—Sushanta Kumar Kar

Choudwar (Lat. 20 33 N. Long. 85 55 E.) is situated on the north bank of river Birupa, a branch of the river Mahanadi, opposite to the Cuttack city. It is 5 km. from Cuttack via Mahanadi-Birupa barrage and 12 km. via Manguli on the N.H.- 5 and N.H.- 42, which passes through the town. The nearest railway station is Nirgundi.

The place assumed prominence under the Somavamsi rule, when Janmejaya Mahabhavagupta occupied it. Choudwar continued to be the hub of political affairs till the late medieval period. This area is rich in varied archaeological remains. Choudwar seems to have contained originally a number of temples, but presently all these are in utter ruins lying scattered in and around the adjoining villages of Agrahat, Kapileswar, Uttareswar and Kedareswar.

The ruins of the fortress lying scattered is one of the biggest among the five forts (*Pancha Katakas*) built by Chodagangadeva of the Ganga dynasty. One large mound (7 m. high and diameter being 40 m.) at the center of fort has eight number of pillars and appears to have possessed antiquities. Recently, Bhubaneswar Circle of Archaeological Survey of India excavated the mound with a view to understand its archaeological remains. I had an opportunity to participate in the excavation in the year 2004-2005. The result of the excavation is described briefly.

The mound is locally known in different names viz., Badhi, Biratagadi, Parabhadi and Ragadi. Prior to excavation the site was visited by a numbers of scholars like R.P. Chanda, P. Acharya, K.C. Panigrahi and N.K. Sahu in the past. During their explorations they could only collect samples, artifacts pertaining to archaeological remains from this locality. They were of the opinion that the mound might contain the remains of a large Buddhist stupa, which was subsequently raised to a considerable height and reused as a pillared hall. During the recent excavation it was observed that, the southwest corner of the mound was dug and destroyed by the treasure hunters long ago.

The excavation has laid bare two structural phases i.e. Phase-I and II. In Phase-I, the lower part of a square temple has been brought to light. The temple has two entrances in east and west with an open *pradakshinapatha*/platform (which is not visible now) with a common foundation of the temple and the platform. The working level of both the temple and the *pradksinapatha*/ platform are in the one and the same stratum. The exterior surface of the basement of temple is carved with usual temple mouldings like *pabhaga* projections in low relief. The *pabhaga* (lower part) has five mouldings, i.e. *khura, kumbha, pata, kani* and *basanta*, while the inner side is plain and simple devoid of any carvings. Two niches are found inside the temple in northern and southern walls. The decorative doorjambs and the entrance sill of the temple might have been removed before filling up the temple with earth/mud during Phase-II. The impression of the doorjambs and entrance sill stone are still found on the eastern and western walls. Neither any deity nor any platform/impression was found from the excavation.

The temple was built with dressed laterite blocks. Sand stones were also used at the eastern entrance. Besides, a few reused stones were utilized in the temple. The extant height of the temple is 2m; the thickness of the wall being 1m. The sanctum sanctorum measures 5 sq.m. In all probability the temple was built during Ganga period. In Phase-II, the temple was found filled up with loose earth and the walls are erected over the *pradakshinapatha*/platform to enlarge the temple.

Two parallel walls with central projection belonging to both Phases-I and II were found. In Phase-I the projected walls might have been served as a terraced platform or an open hall with wall or pillars of low height. A few remains of pillar bases and octagonal pillar shafts have also been unearthed from the excavation. The remains indicate the existence of roof of the structure, which subsequently collapsed.

After collapse/demolition of the structure, subsequently it was required to fill the remains to raise the height of the working level of the temple and expand the structure by way of constructing wall on the *pradakshinapatha*/platform. Again, the exterior surface of the parallel outer wall was decorated with mouldings like that of Phase-I counter part.

Traces of lime plasters on reused stones have been found. To corroborate this, the inscriptional evidence mentions about the sudden shifting of the capital from Choudwar to Barabati fort; there after this place came in to disuse and was abandoned.

After a long gap, some local sadhus frequented this place and one of them erected wooden structure on the available post-holes found in northern and southern walls of the structure support this proposition. Apart these, a lot of hand made iron nails were collected from the debris.

During excavation no sculpture was discovered. Although, a large number of Buddhist sculptures were collected from surface by different scholars in the past.

Pottery : The Red and Grey wares were encountered from digging. The Grey ware is predominant pottery. Their shapes include jar, vase, basin, bowls, dish, handi, knobbed lid, spouted pot, carinated handi and miniature pot, etc.

Besides, a large number of pottery are also found from the surface. These were mainly Red ware, Red slipped ware and Grey ware. Their main shapes are single and double spouted vessels, decorated pots, dishes, etc. The common decorations include pinched, appliquê, thumb impressed designs, etc. On the decoration and style the sherds are assignable to early medieval period.

Terracotta Tiles : Two types of terracotta tiles were encountered during the excavation i.e. of Red and Grey ware. The main shapes of tiles are square, rectangular, oval and 'L' shape.

Both the pottery and the tiles found from the excavation were one and the same with those of Ratnagiri excavation and hence suggesting contemporaneity of both the sites.

Other Archaeological Evidences at Coudwar :

During the excavation I had a chance to explore the other archaeological remains both inside and outside localities of the Choudwar fort, viz., Bharandi, Tokeijhada, Uttareswar temple, Kedareswar Mahadev temple, Narabudi, Baideswar, Rock-cut moat and Rock-cut caves etc.

Bharandi : Bharandi, a rectangular mud fort measuring 2km.X 1km is located 3km. to the south of the Badhi. The height of rampart of the mud fort is about 10 m. above the surroundings. From the surface study it was observed that at the center there was a water reservoir and the habitation was around the reservoir. Remains of three temples have also been noticed to the western side of the reservoir. A portion of laterite retaining wall of the mud rampart was exposed by the stone robbers at the north-west corner of the fort. At present the small river Gandha flows through the mud fort. The remains of the same laterite wall were also exposed inside the riverbed. This fort might have been constructed during the early historical period. Grey and Red ware sherds are plentily available on the surface. Some scholars opine that it was an ancient water reservoir. Whether it is an ancient reservoir containing the temple remains or wall remains inside the water reservoir needs thorough archaeological investigation.

Tokeijhada : The Tokeijhada mound is located on the southern side of the Bharandi. It measures about 6m. high from the surrounding level. The mound contains remains of temples of khondalite stone. The temples might have been constructed during the $10^{th}/11^{th}$ cent. A.D.

Kedareswar Mahadeva temple : Kedareswar temple located 1km. to the east of Badhi, dedicated to Lord Śiva is facing east. Inside the *garbhagriha* the *yonipitha* is without Lingam. The superstructure of the *jagamohana* is missing. Where as upper part of the temple is built with laterite blocks, the lower part is of sand stones. Probably the edifice was renovated in subsequent period. The earlier the superstructure of the temple was constructed with sand stones. Subsequently when the superstructure of the temple fell down or was demolished by the invaders.

Uttareswara Temple : The temple is dedicated to Lord Śiva. Its lower part was built of sand stones, where as the upper part is of laterite stones like that of Kedareswar temple. It also met its end with demolition or crumble down.

Narabudi : Narabudi mound located 0.5km. to north-west of Kedareswara temple is a rich in architectural remains of a temple of sand stones. Though its architectural members are missing; but a part of the *prakara* wall still peeping through the Banian tree root. This temple might have been demolished/ collapsed.

Archaeological evidences of Narabudi might have been the victim of the Muslim inroads in *c.* 14th cent. A.D. Later on, some temples were reconstructed by the then ruling families.

Baideswar temple : The Baideswar temple located 2km. to the north of Badhi is dedicated to Lord Śiva. Inside the *garbhagriha* the *yonipitha* is without Lingam like that of the Kedareswar Mahadeva temple. Its present superstructure is a new one. A few sculptural remains lying within the temple complex belong to the Somavamsi period.

Rock-cut moat : The rock cut moat running all around the fort with a view to protect from wild animals especially elephant and enemy, measures about 6 m. in width and 6m. in depth. It starts from the river Birupa and later joined with the same river. The moat also served as a lifeline for transportation of stones for the construction of temples and for the water management.

Rock-Cut caves : There are three rock-cut caves located in a hillock known as Indrani Pahara. The Buddhist monks in ancient times might have used these caves.

My special thanks to the Superintending Archaeologist, Bhubaneswar Circle of Archaeological Survey of India for his kind suggestions and permission.

REFERENCES

* Assistant Archaeologist, Archaeological Survey of India, Bhubaneswar Circle

1. Behuria, N.C. 1992 *Orissa District Gazetteers*, Cuttack
2. Behera, K.S. 1991 *Kataka (Cuttack) in legends and inscriptions,* Cuttack, 1000 years, pp. 429-437
3. Chanda, R.P. 1930 *Exploration in Orissa, Memoirs of the Archaeological Survey of India,* No. 44, pp. 20-23
4. Panigrahi, K.C. 1995 *History of Orissa*
5. Rajguru, S.N. 1991 *The Age of Cuttack city*, in K.S.Behera, et.al. (ed.), Cuttack 1000 years, pp. 198-205
6. Roy, R. 2005 *"Biratagadira Pratnatatwika Khanana"* (in Oriya) Choudwar Patra, pp.1-6
7. Rao, K.V.B. 2000 Excavation at Barabati Fort, in K.K.Basa, et.al. (ed.), Archaeology of Orissa, pp.663-680.
8. Sinha, B.K. 1991 *Excavation at Barabati Fort, Cuttack, Orissa,* 1989-91, in K.S. Behera, et.al. (ed.), Cuutack 1000 years, pp. 59-68
9. Trivedi, P.K., et. al. 2004-05 *Excavation at Barabati Fort, Cuttack, Orissa* (2003-2004), in "History Today", Journal of Historical Archaeology, No. 5, pp. 86-88.

11

PETROGLYPH SITES IN RAJASTHAN

—Dr. Murari Lal Sharma[1], Madan Lal Meena[2] and Vineet Godhal[3]

Rajasthan is the largest state of the Republic of India in terms of area. It encompasses most of the area of the large, inhospitable Great Indian Desert (Thar Desert), which has an edge paralleling the Sutlej-Indus river valley along its border with Pakistan. The region borders Pakistan in the west, Gujarat in the southwest, Madhya Pradesh in the southeast, Uttar Pradesh, Haryana and Delhi in the northeast, and Punjab, to the north. Rajasthan covers an area of 342,269 sq km.This state is loc^ted in the north-western part of India between 23° 3' to 30° 12' north latitudes and 69° 30' to 78° 17' east longitudes. The state has a rhomb-shaped land with north-south and east-west diagonals, the former measuring about 830 km and the latter about 860 km in length.

Geologically the state is highly varied and complex, revealing the co-existence of the most ancient rocks of Pre-Cambrian age and the most recent alluvium as well as wind-blown sand. The Aravalli, one of the most ancient mountains in the world, have the oldest granite and gneissic rocks at their base, overlain by the rocks of the Aravalli Super group, Delhi Super group, the Vindhyan Super group and younger rocks. These rocks are highly metamorphosed at certain places and show rich occurrences of minerals of great commercial importance.

The Aravalli hill ranges, oldest mountains of India constitute the most dominant hilly area of Rajasthan. The ranges run diagonally across the state from north-east to south-west up to the plains of Gujarat, covering a distance of about 692 kms. Within Rajasthan, the ranges run from Khetri in the north-east to Khed Brahma in the south-west for a length of about 550 kms. In the north-east, the hill ranges

1. Dr. Murari Lal Sharma, Head, Deptt. of History, Govt. P. G. College, Kotputli, Jaipur, Rajasthan-303108
2. Madan Lal Meena, Lecturer in History, Govt. P. G. College, Neemkathana, Sikar, Rajasthan-332713
3. Vineet Godhal, Research Scholar, University of Rajasthan, Jaipur

1) Kanyadeh
2) Viratnagar
3) Sohanpura
4) Kujota
5) Bajni Bhat at Harsora
6) Khola Dungari Hill
7) Bajnibhat at Guhala
8) Chattaneshwar
9) Morajhari
10) Modabhata
11) Koteshwar Mahadeo Hill
12) Astoli
13) Kala Tol

Fig. 11.1. Distribution of Petroglyph Sites in Rajasthan

become more prominent near Khetri and Alwar. Towards the south-west, the ranges become more prominent with peaks upto 1055 m above MSL. It is also a major water divide.

In northern part much of the Ganganagar district is occupied by vast alluvial Ghaggar flood plains. Canals have been constructed through almost all the dry valleys, making the lands around them very productive. The important canal systems are the Ganga canal system, the Bhakra canal system, the west Yamuna canal system and the Indira Gandhi canal system. However, problems of water logging and salinity have also come up at places. The most notable examples are between Suratgarh and Anupgarh. Low sand dunes and sandy hummocks are scattered distributed on the deep sandy alluvial plains in this zone. Barchans have appeared in some parts of the plains because of deep ploughing of the soil without assured supply of canal water.

The eastern plains have rich alluvial soils drained by seasonal rivers. This plain is divided into two physiographic units, (a) Banas Basin or Mewar Plain, and (2) The Chappan Plain. The region of Mewar plain covers the eastern part of Udaipur, Bhilwara, Tonk, Jaipur, western Sawai Madhopur and the southern part of Alwar. The topography of this area is marked by various types of erosional features, produced in the granite and gneiss rocks while the Chappan Plain presents a very different set of landforms.

Southern and south-eastern Rajasthan is mostly a plateau. The Hadauti plateau, having intrusions of black volcanic rocks into the Vindhyans, extends to a great part in Jhalawar, Baran and Kota districts. The Malwa plateau also extends into the southern part of Chittaurgarh and Banswara districts having an average altitude of 500 m above MSL and is dotted with isolated low ranges at few places. This plateau in Rajasthan occurs in the upper catchment of the Chambal river to the south-east of the Mewar plains. The greater part of this area is drained by the river Chambal and its tributaries like Kali Sindh, Parwan and Parvati.

The Luni Jawai plain occurs in the district of Jodhpur, Pali, Jalore, Sirohi, and in the southern part of the Nagaur. It contain the only integrated drainage system in the Thar Desert. The Luni originates near Ajmer and flows south-westward to the great Rann of Kutch. Its tributaries are ephemeral and have wide sandy beds.

The Shekhawati tract is in Jhunjhunu, Sikar and Churu districts and northern part of Nagaur district. This zone has very few streams, most of which disappears after flowing for short distances in the sandy plains. The important streams are Mendha and Rupangarh which originate in the Aravalli hill ranges and drain into the Sambhar salt lake. The other major stream Kantli flows north-westwards from Aravallis and disappear in the sandy plains near Rajgarh.

There were fairly dense forest in the range of Aravalli, but due to rapid increase in population, a great deal of forest has been destroyed. In the district of Udaipur, Dungarpur, Bansawara, Chittauragarh, Kota and Jhalawar, *teak* or *sagwan* (*Tectona grandis*) is the predominant tree. Another common tree is *mahua* (*Bassia latifolia /Madhuca indica*). Outside the Aravallis, the vegetation cover in the plains is quite thick. Near the villages, *aam* (*Mangifera indica*), *pipal* (*Ficus religiosa*), *ber* (*Ficus bengalensis*), *gular* (*Ficus glomerata*), *jamun* (*Eugenia jambolena*), and tamarind (*Tamarindus indica*) are common. In the fields, *babul* (*Acacia arabica*), *khajur* (*Phoenix sylvestris*), and *dhak* or *palas* (*Butea frondosa*), *khejri* (*Prosopis spicigera*) are common. The flora is more varied than that of the region to its north. Among the more common trees are *aam*, *babul*, *jamun*, *khair* (*Acacia catechu*), *khajur*, *khejri*, *mahua*, *pipal* and *ranjura* (*Acacia leucophlea*). The less common trees are *bahera* (*Terminalia bellerica*), *dhaman* (*Grewia oppositifolia*) *dhao*, *haldu* (*Adina cordifolia*) *hingota* (*Balanites roxburghit*), *kachnar* (*Bauhinia purpurea*) etc. *Bamboo* (*Dendrocalamus strictus*) is found only in the hills. The most important among the food plants are *Khejri, ker, kumat,ber, khajur*, *jal*, *kankera*, *karela*, *kheenp*, *matira*, *phog* and *bhurant*.

In the Aravalli hills, till the early part of the last century, the tiger (*Panthera tigris*), black bear (*Melursus ursinus*), and sambhar (*Cervus unicolor*) were common. The Sariska sanctuary, located in the Alwar district has dry deciduous jungle, interspersed with scrubs. Wildlife in the sanctuary comprises leopard, tiger, jungle cat, caracal, rusty spotted cat, civet, wolf, jackal (*Canis aureus*), mongoose (*Herpestes edwardsi*), wild boar, nilgai (*Boselphus tragocamelus*), chital, sambhar, chowsingha (*Tetracerus quadricornis*), hare (*Lepus nigricollis*), porcupine (*Hystrix indica*), langur (*Presbytis entellus*) and over 200 species of birds. The Keoladeo Ghana sanctuary in Bharatpur district receives a very large number of migratory birds from central Asia and Europe during winter. Elsewhere also common birds can be seen in all parts of the state.

Archaeologically, the state of Rajasthan is very rich. It was in the seventies of the nineteenth century that C.A. Hackett of the G.S.I. had made a surface collection of palaeoliths from Jaipur, Bundi and Indergarh. After 1950, H.D.Sankalia, S.R. Rao, M.N. Deshpande, A.P. Khatri, K.V. Soundara Rajan and V.N. Misra made substantial contributions in this field. Misra's (Misra, 1961) explorations on Banas, Berach and Luni basins added a lot to our knowledge of stone age complex in Rajasthan. Palaeolithic tools have been reported from Pali, Barmer, Jaisalmer, Bikaner,

Nagaur, Jodhpur, Udaipur, Chittaurgarh, Jaipur, Alwar, Sikar, Jhunjhunu, Sirohi, Kota and Sawaimadhopur districts. It has been also conceived that during the Middle Palaeolithic period the river Luni in western Rajasthan was perennial. The discovery of Mesolithic sites in different parts of Rajasthan is very interesting in as much that dozens of such sites have recently been discovered even in Jaipur, Alwar, Sikar and Jhunjhunu districts, all along the river beds of Kantli, Sahibi, Sota, Dohan and Kansawati (Sharma, M.L. 1997).

In the field of rock art, it was the cold season of 1867-68, when the first discovery of the Stone Age rock painting was made in India. This discovery was done by Archibald Carlleyle; who found some paintings in a few rock shelters at Sohagighat in the district of Mirzapur. Carlleyle was the first man in the world who associated these paintings with prehistoric people and whose physical and cultural remains he had excavated from these shelters. Thus not only the first prehistoric paintings were discovered in India but the idea of their prehistoric antiquity was also conceived firstly.

India is one of the very rich zones of prehistoric rock art. Central India and Vindhyan sandstone belt is studded with several thousand painted rock shelters. Two-thirds of pictographic sites are located in this belt. There is a 60 kilometer semi-circular belt in the source region of the Betwa near Bhopal which has some 45 big concentrations of painted rock shelters. Bhimbetka, the famous site of Indian rock painting is located at the centre of the belt.

In 1877, H. Rivett Carnac (Carnac, 1877) published an article on ancient sculpturing on rocks in the Journal of the Asiatic society of Bengal. Carnac found cup-marks of different sizes and depths on rocks located some 200 meters south of the Chandreshwar temple at Dwarhat in the district of Almora. Some early historic petroglyphs were noticed by A.H. Franke (Franke, 1902) in the lower Ladakh region before one hundred years ago. The distribution of petroglyphs is far widely spread than pictographs. In the north, they are noticed in Kargil, Leh and Ladakh region while in the north-west, engravings occur at four places at he bank of Indus river. Some petroglyph sites are located in Himachal Pradesh, Rajasthan, Orissa, Meghalaya and also in Manipur.

Sohanpura is a Chalcolithic type rock art site of Ganeshwar-Jodhpura culture. Lower Palaeolithic tools were collected from the foot hill of the Sohanpura. Chalcolithic antiquities like rings, Chisels, rods etc. were also collected from here. A small village, Dhundhana, which yielded chalcolithic pottery, chalcopyrities and slag, a Chalcolithic site, is located 2 km away in north direction from Bajni Bhat.

Petroglyphs are pecked by sharp pointed stones. No chisel was necessary to obtain thin battered points. The south Indian petroglyphs are also the result of pecking by harder stones.

The technique of execution is by using hammer stones. Indian cupules are executed on very hard quartzite and also on other rock types like marble, granite and sandstone depending upon the geological location. The cup marks are mostly found on the surface of the wall of the rock shelters.

What was the motivation behind the creation of rock art in Indian context is still an enigma. Some critical interpretations have been given by scholars about the meaning and aim of the rock art. Wakankar and Brooks stated that no single explanation can be given for the motivation of this multifarious form of rock art. There may be different reasons in different context of this art. The large sized animal's drawings were painted for worship after or before killing the actual animal. Probably the hunting scenes were inspired by hunting magic. Scenes of day to day activities and some of the paintings might have been drawn simply for purposes of decoration.

Rock art sites are the cultural centers not only of prehistoric age but also of protohistoric and historic period. Cupules or cup-marks are probably the most common form of petroglyph in the world. Some of the scholars believe that it is a form of rock art (Bednarik, 2000-2001). It is assumed by the scholars that these cupules were made for the similar purposes and may be possible that some of those found on horizontal surfaces were used for other purposes. The dots, shallow impressions, cup marks found in Indian rock art were probably a part of the specimen of utilitarian art. Cup marks or cupules are found in simple rows, U-shaped and in linear pattern and also without any definite arrangement. Mostly cupules or cup-marks occur in groups, often numbering in their hundred or single pattern. Mountford (1976:213) who saw the making of cupules in Central Australia during 1940, reports that these depressions were made as increased ritual for the Pink Cockatoo. From Southern Kenya, where Odak (1988) has described geometric assemblages of cupules, reported an ethenographic example of non-ceremonial cupules. They are claimed to have been used in board games such as the *boa* game, but in that area, cupules were used also for other purposes.

In Peninsular India, petroglyphs are found on the granite boulders which are heaped together to form small hillocks. The gray colour rock provides a suitable canvas for the execution of abraded drawings.

Till 1989, no petroglyphs were recorded from central India but in 1990, eleven petroglyphs (Bednarik, 1991) were observed in Auditorium Cave in Bhimbetka, which consist entirely of rock paintings. Two of the petroglyphs, a cupule and a meandering line had been excavated by V.S. Wakankar in an acheulian deposit directly covering them. Other nine cupule, although found above the ground, are almost certainly of similar age (Bednarik 1996). Remaining nine cupules are located on the vertical panel of a huge boulder on the floor of the cave called Chief's Rock. Michel Lorblanchet, an Australian specialist of cave art examined the cupules in 1990 and judged them to be natural rock markings rather than petroglyphs. Daraki-Chattan, a small narrow cave in the quartzitic buttresses of Indragarh hill in Tehsil Bhanpura, district Mandsaur, Madhya Pradesh is now a well known cupule site in the country, was discovered by Ramesh K. Pancholi (Pancholi, 1994) in 1993. The archaeological excavation was conducted here to obtain evidences related with the creation of cupule at this site. Cupules or cup marks are a universal phenomenon in rock art tradition of the world, and are presumed to be the most numerous of all petroglyph motifs. They occur in all continents except Antartica. The oldest cupules found in the Africa, Australia, Canada and Europe. Cupules have been dated 50,000 years BP also in Australia.

Rock art in Rajasthan

So far, considerable work has been done in the field of rock art in Rajasthan. Aravalli range, which divides the state into two unequal parts, has been playing an important role in the development of economic and cultural life of the people since prehistoric times.

From the eastern part of the state, more than 100 rock art sites have been recorded by scholars. Chambal valley is the most important area from the view of rock art study. In 1979, first rock art site was reported by Dr. V.S. Wakankar and their student Giriraj Kumar (Kumar, 1981) and Ramesh K. Pancholi from the district of Kota and Baran in the valley of Chambal river. Some rock art sites were discovered by Shri Vijai Shankar Srivastav and Shri Jagat Narayan Srivastav (Srivastav, 1981) from Upper Chambal Valley. Some exploration work has been done by Dr. M.L. Sahu in Kota district, Shri Tejsingh and Shri Omprakash Sharma "Kukki" (Kukki, 1998) in the area of Bundi district. In 1989, a joint survey was done by Department of History, Government College, Neemkathana and the State Department of Archaeology and Museums, Government of Rajasthan, (Sharma *et al*, 1992) of North-East Rajasthan. In last decade, a general survey of rock art sites have been done in the districts of Jaipur, Sikar, Jhunjhunu, Alwar, Bharatpur, Dausa, Sawai Madhopur, Pali, Jodhpur, Sirohi, Chittaurgarh, Bhilwara, Kota, Bundi, Jhalawar, Sirohi etc.

More than 100 pictograph sites are discovered in Rajasthan in which more than 10 sites having petroglyphs.

Petroglyph Sites in Rajasthan

Petroglyphs may be divided into five groups called engraving, carving, bruising, dotting and cup-marking. In Rajasthan, two types of petroglyphs have been discovered (1) Engraving, and (2) Cupule. Engravings occur in the form of line drawings, incised on rocks, while a cupule or cup-mark is a depression, executed on natural rock surfaces. The shapes of the cupules may be circular or elliptical. It also varies in depth and diameter. These cup-marks are found in dots, shallow depressions in simple rows,u-shaped and necklace-shaped compositions and also without definite arrangements. Engravings have been discovered from Sohanpura, Kanyadeh, Viratnagar, and Kujota while cupules are reported from Kanyadeh, Koteshwar Mahadeo hill, Chattaneshwar, Sohanpura, Morajhari, Modabhata, Kalapahad, Astoli, Viratnagar, Khola Dungri hill, Guhala (Fig.1) etc.

(1) Kanyadeh

Kanyadeh is situated near Bilasgadh, a small village in the district of Baran. This site falls under the Vindhyan plateau with thorny trees, scrub and vines digging to the rock and stream far bellow. These rock shelters range in size from 15 meter long, 5 meter deep and 6 meter high. Most of them fall generally in between the streams. Petroglyphs have been discovered in the form of a deep carved line, which is probably made by pecking on the floor of the rock shelter KNDH III A, on the river Bilasi. In 1991, cupules have been discovered at this site by Dr. Giriraj Kumar, Ramesh K. Pancholi and Nirdeep Roy (Kumar *et al,* 1992). Cupules are in the form of a combination of cupules or a few independent cupules. These irregularly distributed cupules have been seen on the floor of the rock shelter.

(2) Viratnagar

Bairath or Viratnagar (27° 24.56' North, 76°12' East) of Mahabharata period, located some 80 kms north of Jaipur on Delhi highway. This place has been a famous Buddhist centre during the early historic period and is surrounded by fine quality granite hills. There are three hills namely Ganesh Dungari, Bheem Dungari and Beejak Dungri. In the foot of Ganesh temple hill, the site museum of the Department of Archaeology and Museums, Government of Rajasthan located. By the side of the temple, and above the museum, there is a complex of rough grained huge granite rocks which were parts of the once single giant rock. This rock shelter complex holds a strategic position in the area and commands a panoramic view of the valley. These rock shelters have deposit containing early historic pottery, hence appears to have been used by monks and sagas in early historic period (Kumar and Sharma, 1995). Now days these shelters also appear to have been used for preparation for food for picnic parties. What is important to note is that water channels have been cut into the shelter floor to check the rain water coming on the floor (Plate 1). At the mouth of the rock shelter curved channel has been cut on the floor slopping backwards. Another small curved channel is meeting it inside the mouth of the shelter to its right side. The mouth of the shelter is 4 meter wide and 1.5 meter high. The big quartz crystals and black chips of minerals form important constituents of the rock. The big channel is comparatively wider on the floor surface and narrow on the bottom with slightly outward tilting sides. Near the mouth of the shelter it is carved, comparatively narrow with almost U shaped cross section and almost unweathered. Its dimensions are :

Width on the floor: 6.0 cm

Width at the bottom: 3.0 cm

Depth 2.7 cm

Inside the shelter, it is weathered at places and comparatively bigger in dimensions.

Width on the floor: 13 to 11.50 cm

Width at the bottom: 9 to 8.50 cm

Depth: 4.93 to 3.25 cm

The other small channel is weathered. It dimensions are:

Width: 9.5 cm

Depth: 2.5 to 2.3 cm

Such chisel cut channels have also been discovered in Madana-Ki-Khoh shelter at Madanpura near Fatehpur Sikari in Uttar Pradesh and in early Buddhist cave at Karle in Maharashtra.

There are two chisel carved cup marks with flaring sides and flat floor are observed. Their dimensions are:

1. 19.5 x 18.5 x 3.15 cm
2. 9.5 x 8.5 x 1.9 cm

There are three more cup marks in front of the big rock shelter.

(3) Sohanpura

Sohanpura (27° 49.5' North, 75° 58.5' East) is a small village in the Sikar district of Rajasthan (Sharma, 1994). The site is situated in the formation of sandstone, 2 km east of the village and about 0.5 km north of river Kasawati, which is a perennial river.

The site is called as "Payga" by the local villagers. Sometimes it is called as "Suraj-Chand ki Dhad". This Payga hill is surrounded by Aravalli range from east, west and southern direction. Sohanpura is a type rock art site of Ganeshwar-Jodhpura Chalcolitic Culture. A habitation mound is located 2 km away from the Rock art site which yielded Ganeshwar-Jodhpura pottery and some other cultural material. The mound is almost 10 meter high from surrounding level. The hill is formed by micaceous sandstone of Alwar formation. There are 7 rock shelters located in this hill but five shelters have pictographs.

A big shelter is located in the foothill which sized 20 meter length, 2 meter wide and 5 meter high. This shelter is divided into two unequal parts by the flow of water. Paintings have been eroded and destroyed due to flow of water in left portion. Most of the engravings are done on the vertical surface of the rock shelter. The figures are shown in isolation in a free standing pose. Among these figures, two humped bull are made by pecking technique with different style.

Another shelter is located on the top of the hill; 70 meter long, 6 meter wide and 11 meter high. Three humped bull and two human figures are made by same technique (plate 2). The third figure is not clear.

Technically all the engravings were made by pecking technique. Some of the figures are in realistic position.

Another shelter is located on the top of the hill in north-east direction of the upper mentioned shelter. The shelter is comparatively smaller compared to the rest of the shelters. Some stone slabs have been used to make the floor inside the shelter. These stone slabs are arranged in circular pattern. It is a big platform prepared by erecting a wall in front of the shelter and filling the space in between by the soil and stone pieces. Later this platform was raised in two successive phases by erecting stone walls in front of the shelter. But in each phase the wall was shifted closer to the shelter. Thus platform represents three phases of its construction and elevation.

A big stone slab is lying on the platform near the stone wall. Inside the rock shelter, on the platform of the third phase, which forms the present floor of the rock shelter, some rough and almost circular cup marks (plate 3) are observed encircling of big stone slabs. Ten cupules are arranged in two almost parallel lines on one piece of stone slab. Due to the long span of the time, upper portion of the cup marks (1.45 mm) have been eroded. Another stone slab bears four deep cup marks 4 to 6 cm in diameter and 6.0 to 8.3 mm in depth. They have been arranged in a row on one side of the stone. These are with deep pecking marks and rough in execution. Dimension of this stone slab is different from both corners.

(4) Kujota

Kujota is a small village of Kotputli sub-division, in the district of Jaipur, located 9 km away from Goverdhanpura Chowki in western direction, which is 13 km away from Kotputli on Kotputli-Jaipur road, National highway no. 8. There are so many small hillocks of lime stone around this village. Presently mining of limestone is being by Rajasthan Mines Development Corporation. Another village Bhainslana, which is not far away from Kujota, thick deposit of black marble can be seen here. Extraction of black marble is being done since medieval period. Both villages are located on the bank of Sota River, which is a main tributary of Sahibi River. The height of small hillocks vary between 100-200 feet. Lime stone is comparatively shofter sand stone. Different motives can be engraved easily from a hard stone tool or any pointed metal equipment.

On way to Ajetpura-Bhainslana, in south-western direction, in the field of Mitthan Kanjar, a wedge shape rock was situated with some elevation from the surface. Dimension of this rock was 5x6 meter. Every space was used for depiction of historical scene on this rock. A camel rider with sword in one hand and shield in another was depicted by the artist. Two human figures with same weapons were engraved both sides of this cavalier. In other motifs, a warrior, elephant, horse, camel were also depicted (plate 7). This panel was the biggest panel of Kujota petroglyph site. Now this rock has been destroyed by the workers during the mining work.

Another small rock is located near upper mentioned rock at the height of 30-40 cm from the surface. Three human figures are made on the flat surface of this rock. The figures are in standing position (plate 4) with warrior's uniform. The longest figure's dimension is 38x21 cm. it has sword in one hand and shield in the other. One elephant rider is also depicted on this panel.

200 meter away from the first rock, another rock is located with the depiction

of 'Char-Bhar'. Some villagers also play this game for their entertainment during their rest time. Size of this petroglyph is 29x50 cm.

In the south-east direction of the village, a rock shelter is located in the middle of the hill with some engravings on the flat surface of the rock. In this group, a warrior with a sword and a shield is depicted. Some human figures are depicted with arms in their hands in standing position. Elephants, horse and some others animals are depicted in different postures. A camel rider is also depicted in this group.

Some other engravings were also observed on the nearby rocks abut due to weathering, they could not be identified.

(5) Bajni Bhat at Harsora

Bajni Bhat, (27° 46.8' North, 76° 26.9' East) which means 'ringing rock' or 'rock that gives sound; i.e. lithophone' (Kumar *et al* 2005) is located near Harsora in Tehsil Bansur of Alwar district. This site was discovered by M.L. Sharma and late Shri P.T. Sharma in 1991 (Sharma *et al,* 1992) which is a lower palaeolithic cupule site. Petroglyph site is located near Jhirna in the granite hill which is locally known as "Kalapahad". Acheulian tools were collected from the Jhirna nala during the exploration. Bajni Bhat is a granite rock. Its front portion bears a shelter facing North-west with an orientation 40° north East and 20° South-west.

Most of the cupules in the rockshelter have been executed on the vertical wall (plate 5). The cupules are on the plain unexfoliated surface. Eight cupules out of the total 66 are aligned along the edge of the big fractured rock. They are comparatively very shallow. The cupules on the rock have been executed without any pattern. They are generally round. Scattered strokes can be seen around the shallow cupules. Most of the cupules are quite big in size varying between 65 x 65 x 4.4 mm to 110 x 90 x 10.4 mm. They are almost circular in shape. The cupules are finely executed and their surface appears smooth. Some micro depressions also can be observe around the cupules. It is due to the weathering of weak minerals. Light red colour deposit with small stone pieces of chert can be seen on the floor. Few acheulian scrapers, handaxes and middle palaeolithic tools and some flakes on chert were also obtained during the exploration.

(6) Khola Dungari Hill

Near Kalapahar (27° 45' North, 76° 25' East) surrounded by Jhirana and Toli Dungri, is Khola (Sharma *et al,* 1992), there is a big rock of Granite located about

100 meters away from Jhirna shelter. This rock contains petroglyph. It is a depression of about 3.5 cm in depth and about 11 cm in diameter. Possibly this stone was used as a musical stone which is certainly of lithophone type.

(7) Bajni Bhat at Guhala

Guhala is a small village on the Neemkathana-Sikar road, 25 kilometer away from Nemmkathana in southern direction. A small village which is called as "Ugrawala ki Dhani" is located two kilometer away from Guhala in Southwest direction of the right bank of the Kantli river. A small hill is located 150 meter away in the south direction of this village. This site is one kilometer from Karanpura in east and 2 kilometer east of Narsinghpuri, which is a Chalcolithic site of Ganeshwar-Jodhpura culture. More than 17 stone slabs have been seen on the hill which bears more than 200 cup marks of different dimensions (plate 6 & 8). These varied shape stone slabs called "Bajni Bhat" by local people which means "Rock that gives sound". The frontal view is very beautiful bowl shaped valley with fertile land. Some sand stone and marble mines are located in the eastern part of the hill. Dimension of the hill is 250 x 30 meter. The hill is formed by hard quartzitic sandstone. Some part of the hill is destroyed during the mining work. Cup marks are made of different dimensions and shapes like round, circular, elongated, oval, shallow, etc. Their size varies between 25 x 25 x 5 mm to 150 x 120 x 18 mm.

It is really surprising that more than 200 cup marks are recorded from Guhala but no tool was found in the nearby area. It may be possible that during the mining work, tools got disturbed under the mines.

(8) Chattaneshwar

Chattanshwar is a small village located 20 km south of Kota near Cablenagar on the bank of Alnia river. Almost 70 cupules have executed on the bedrock of a rock shelter at this site in Chambal valley. Cupules have been arranged into two different manners: 1) an ovoid form (35 x 50 cm), and 2) a 'U' form with its arm curved rightward and having a small line inside at its bottom. Their diameter varies between 21 x 20 mm to 25.5 x 25.5 mm and depth from 2 to 2.5 mm. some light brown patination can also be seen on the cupules.

However, Chattaneshwar and Kanyadeh cupule belongs to one category but at Chattaneshwar development of cupule's pattern can be observed.

(9) Morajhari

Morajhari is a small village in Sapanda panchayat of Nasirabad in Ajmer district (Kumar, 1998) 20 km east of Nasirabad. There are some granite rocks behind the village in the east and southeast direction. There are several hundred boulders which bear cup-marks. The rocks are fine grained, grey in colour with black crystals in it.

Two rocks bear cup marks. The major cupule rock is elongated and roughly roundish in shape. This rock is resting on the bed rock. It is full of cupules on all its faces on the upper and lower surface. The cupules are of different size and shape from small to circular, almost all with smooth surface. The cupule rock lying on the bed rock gives a sweet metallic sound on striking with a stone or a stick. The standing rock also gives a metallic sound.

Another cupule rock-2 is located about 100 meter south wards of cupule rock-1. Comparatively this rock is much bigger, thicker and almost flat in appearance. 200 cup marks are observed on this rock. Some stone pieces are lying around this rock, out of which only a few bear striking marks. No stone implements were collected from this and nearby region.

Morajhari cupule site and its surrounding area indicate that this site is unique in their characters of size, shape, depth and distribution patterns of the cupules.

(10) Moda Bhata

Hathikheda is located about 4 kilometers to the west of Ajmer, having an expense of flat fluvial deposit with dry river courses (Kumar and Bednarik, 2002). Hathikheda, an outer suburb of greater Ajmer, one of the major population centers of Rajasthan. The word 'Hathikheda' means 'Elephant Village.' A series outcrops, spaced about one kilometer apart, extends to the west of the built-up-area, forming a roughly discernible alignment along the east west line. They rise between eight and twenty meters above the alluvium and consist essentially of white quartz monoliths.

The second outcrop is called 'Moda Bhata' which is located immediately north of a usually dry watercourse, on the present periphery of the town. Twenty cupules are seen on this platform. Most of the cupules occur in small groups. They are located on the slight rise of the rock platform. Some human activities, like abrasion and quarrying, have been observed on the surface of the rock. The largest cupules measure between thirty five and twenty eight centimeters across its rim and it is ten centimeters deep.

About one kilometer to the south-southwest of the Moda Bhata (Kumar et al 2005), lies a very similar formation, called 'Mahadeo Bhata'. Its dimensions and morphology are much like of Moda Bhata, with steep sides and a horizontal platform. Total twenty cupules have been seen on this platform. There is a big rock shelter on this hill, also bearing cupules, some of which are as large as the one in the rock shelter at Moda Bhata.

Not a single readily recognizable stone tool was located, but the search was cursóry and more through examination is essential.

(11) Koteshwar Mahadeo Hill

The site is located to the south of the hill of Moda Bhata cupule site. 3 cupules were discovered by Dr. Giriraj Kumar and Suresh Prajapati (Kumar and Prajapati, 2005) on the top of the quartz hill. There is a big rock shelter measuring 18 meter long, 4 meter in height and 3 meter in depth. There are clusters of cupules on its floor and vertical wall. Total ten cupules have been observed on this shelter. A number of cupules were also observed on the flat rocks, a little away in front of the hill in its west. The cupules are similar to those observed on Moda Bhata rock.

(12) Astoli

This site is located near the district of Bundi. Petroglyph site of Astoli was discovered by Ramesh K. Pancholi last year (Personal communication). A stone slab, 13 feet long, 4 feet wide and more than one feet high, bears more than 60 cup marks. Some cupules are also observed on other stone slabs.

(13) Kala Tol

Kala Tol is a solitary umberalla shape rock shelter which is situated at the western slope of the hill near Budhpura village of Bundi tehsil of Bundi district. This shelter has four groups ff pictographs in which bull, deer, cattles, horse riders, hunter and human figures are depicted. Southern group is relatively rich which has been excavated by the villagers to find out some wealth. In front of these paintings under the shelter there was a rock which has 7 feet vertical surface. On this rock, a circular cup mark is depicted which is highly weathered. It was discovered on 12th December on this year. This site situated at Mala Kanala which is a tributary of Mangli river. Mangli river flows in the Mez river.

Discussion

Most of the sites are located near the hilly areas, where evidences of human activity since prehistoric period to modern period can be observed. These sites are located near rock art sites of prehistoric period. Palaeolithic tools were collected from these sites.

Cupules or cup-marks are a universal feature in the field of petroglyphs in the world. They occurs in all continents except Antartica and it seems that they have been made in most periods of history, beginning with the lower palaeolithic and ending in the middle ages in Europe and in even more recent times in such regions as Australia where their manufacture only ceased in 20th century.

What was the motive of these cup marks? Is it art or not? From which culture they belong? At the present state of our knowledge, we can not say anything definitely. Some scholars have interpreted that these cupules were made during the musical function of the primitive men. This also flashes from the name of the sites like Bajni Bhat (rock that gives sound) and Pola Bhat (rock which is hollow from inside). Some others believe that these cupules are related with some magical function. Some other researchers believe that cupules were made for preparation of paints, for cultic rituals, pounding of medicines, pigments or spices, the placement of offerings, including human blood and semen, depiction of star constellations, depiction of topographic elements of nearby landscapes, board games, a symbolism etc. (Bednarik 2008). Mathpal Says (Mathpal 1995) that presence of cupules on a menhir may represent their association with mortuary rites. Sometimes the space in between two cup marks is maintained geometrically symmetrical. Are these cup marks related with astronomy or metrology? There must have been some significant motives behind deep cup marks. Currently we have no information about the motive of creation of cup marks.

However, to arrive at some conclusion about the development of cupule forms, a systematic study is needed in Indian and also in world context.

References

Bednarik, R.G. 1993. Palaeolithic Art in India. *Man and Environment* 18(2):33-40

Bednarik, R.G., G. Kumar and G.S. Tyagi. 1991. Petroglyphs from Central India. *Rock Art Research* 8:33-35.

Bedbarik, R.G. 1996. The cupules of chief's rock, Auditorium Cave, Bhimbetka. *The Artefact* 19:63-72.

Bednarik, R.G. 2008. Cupules. *Rock Art Research* 2008:61-100.

Carnac, H.R.C.S. 1877. Rough Notes on Some Ancient Sculpturings on rocks in Kumaon, similar to those found on monoliths and rocks in Europe. *Journal of the Asiatic Society of Bengal,* Vol XLVI (1):1-15

Dikshit, K.N., 1966-68. A Note on Palaeolithic Site at Bairath in Rajasthan. *The Researcher* 7-9:26

Franke, A.H.1902. Notes on Rock Carvings from Lower Ladakh. *The Indian Antiquary* Vol. 31:398-401.

Kukki, Omprakash Sharma.1998. Discovery of Rock Paintings in Chhaja river, District Bundi, Rajasthan.*Purakala* 9 (1-2):69-70.

Kumar, Giriraj. 1981. Painted Rock Shelters from Rajasthan in Vijay Prakash Srivastava (ed), *Cultural Contours of India: Dr. Satyaprakash Felicitation Volume.* New Delhi:Abhinav Publications:277-285.

Kumar, G., R.K. Pancholi, S. Nagdev, G.S. Runwal, J.N. Srivastav and J.D. Tripathi. 1992. Rock Art of Upper Chambal Valley Part 1: Rock Art and Rock Art Sites. *Purakala* 3 (1-2):13-55

Kumar, G. 1996. Darki-Chattan: A Palaeolithic Cupule Site in India. *Rock Art Research* 13:38-46

Kumar, G.1998. Morajhari: A Unique Cupule Site in Ajmer District, Rajasthan. *Purakala* 9:61-64

Kumar, G. and M.L. Sharma.1999. Documentation of Cupules on Morajhari Cupule Rocks in Rajasthan, *Purakala* 10(1-2):33-44

Kumar, G and Robert G. Bdnarik, 2002. The Quartz Cupules of Ajmer, Rajasthan, *Purakala* 13(1-2):45-50

Kumar, G. and Suresh Prajapati, 2005. Petroglyphs Discovered in Ajmer, Rajasthan. *Purakala* 14-15:116-117.

Kumar, Giriraj, Robert G. Bednarik, Alan Watchman and Richard G. Roberts. 2005. The EIP Project in 2005: A Progress Report. *Purakala* 14-15:13-68

Kumar Giriraj and Murarilal Sharma. 1995. Petroglyph Sites in Kalapahad and Ganesh-Hill:Documentation and Observations. *Purakala* 6 (1-2):56-59.

Kumar, Giriraj, Robert G. Bednarik, Alan Watchman and Richard G. Roberts. 2005. The EIP Project in 2005:A Progress Report. *Purakala* 14-15:13-68

Misra, V.N. 1967. Pre and Protohistory of Berach Basin. Deccan College Poona.

Mathpal, Yashodhar. 1995. *Rock art in Kumaon Himalaya*. Indira Gandhi National Centre For the Arts and Aryan Books Iternational, New Delhi.

Mountford, C.P. 1976. *Nomads of the Australian desert.* Rigby, Adelaide.

Odak, O. 1988. Cup-marks patterns as an interpretation strategy in some southern Kenyan petroglyphs. In M.Lorblanchet (ed.), *Rock art in the Old World,* pp. 49-60. Indira Gandhi National Centre for the Arts, New Delhi.

Pancholi, Ramesh Kumar. 1994. New Discoveries in Bhanpura Region. *Purakala 5* (1-2):75.

Sharma, Murari lal, Vijay Kumar and P.T. Sharma. 1992. New Rock Art Sites Discovered in Sahibi Valley Rajasthan. *Purakala* 3(1-2):84

Sharma, Murari lal.1994. Sohanpura-Payga Rock Art Site. *Purakala* 5(1-2):73-74

Sharma, M.L.1996. The Sahibee River Valley:A New Region of Rock Art in Rajasthan, in R.K. Sharma and K.K. Tripathi (ed), *Prehistoric Art in India.* New Delhi:Aryan Books International:153-159

Sharma, M.L.1997. Rock Art of Northern Rajasthan. *Purakala* 8 (1-2):25-35.

Sharma, M.L. and M.L. Meena. 2004. Rock Painting in North-East Rajasthan:Content and Significance. *Nucleus* 4(1):47-52

Sharma, M.L. 2005. Shailchitrakala:Uttar Purvee Rajasthan. *Shodh Patrika* 56 (1-4). 5-25.Udaipur: Rajasthan Vidyapeeth.

Sharma, M.L. 2006. Viratnagar Ke Chitrit Shailashrya. *Puratan* 16:116-127. Bhopal

Sharma, M.L, Meena, M.L., Sharma, Rajendra, Godhal Vineet. 2008. *Distribution and structural Characteristics of Petroglyphs of Rajasthan,* Paper presented in the 13th Rock Art Congress held at Indira Gandhi Rastriya Manav Sangrahalya, Bhopal from 31st October-1st November 2008 in association with Rock Art Society of India.

Sharma, Murari lal. 2009. Shail-Chitrakala:Uttar Purvee Rajasthan Ke Vishesh Sandarbh Me Ek Adhyyan in G.L. Badam, S.K. Bajpai and K.K. Chakraverty (ed), *Madhya Bharat Ki Shail-Chitrakala*. New Delhi:B.R. Piblishing Corporation:57-89.

Srivastav, Jagatnarayan. 1981. Alania (Kota) Ke Pragaitihasik Shilashrya Chitra in Vijay Prakash Srivastava (ed), *Cultural Contours of India:Dr. Satyaprakash Felicitation Volume.* New Delhi:Abhinav Publications:329-331.

12

BUDDHIST REMAINS OF CHHATTISGARH: NEED FOR HOLISTIC REASSESSMENT

—J. Manuel

Introduction

This state contiguous with eastern part of Madhya Pradesh shares boundary with Uttar Pradesh, Bihar, Orissa, Andhra Pradesh and Maharashtra. Bestowed with several plains and nourished by the Mahanadi and its tributaries besides Indravati this land is an epitome of natural beauty from time immemorial. The state of Chhattisgarh known so after the proverbial thirty six forts in this region, is provided with variant topography by the hills of Maikal ranges, Chhotta Nagpur; Bastar and Orissa hills. The different geological formations, namely; the Archaeans, Cuddapah, Gondwanas, Lower Cretacean (Sharma 2002 :805,806)and good rains provided different land forms besides nourishment to flora, fauna, and human beings. The evidence of prehistoric cultures is marked by the presence of stone tools from the Lower Palaeolithic to the Mesolithic periods (Pandey 1994: 1-3). Megalithic monuments have also been reported in Bastar region(Jha 1978: 61-65). Besides this from early historic times ancient trade routes passed through this region. Adorned with such early sites like Bodhgaya, Sarnath, Amravati, Ajanta and Sanchi besides Nalanda, Ratnagiri, Lalitgiri, Nagarjunakonda, Ellora, Bagh and Dhamnar in the neighboring states, all assignable to later time brackets, the influence of Buddhism in this region was a natural corallary. Therefore the finding of more than 20 sites with Buddhist remains which were being reported from as early as the later part of 19th century across the entire length and breadth of the state is not surprising. However, these are only part of the entire picture and more sites or at least stray findings will be revealed, eventually as accessibility for the scholars increases. This fact has been established by the recent findings that have come to light from explorations and excavations.

The state has yielded archaeological remains of the Mauryan, Satavahana, Kushan, Magha, rulers with Mitra ending names, Sharabpuriya, Panduvamshi, Kalchuri and others (Tripathi and Mishra1994: p 136). A king Mahendra, is said to have been defeated by Samudragupta of the Imperial Guptas. Evidence of the Gupta rule is surmised from coins attributed to Kumaragupta and Skandagupta (Ahmed 1994: 55). However, contemporary to the Guptas, several kings of the Nala dynasty are known to have ruled in this region. They probably hailed from eastern part of Bastar with their capital at Pushkari. During their zenith, their power extended to Vidharbha. Prithvisena of the Vakatakas had destroyed their hold. However, the Nala inscription tentatively assigned to circa 700 AD shows that the dynasty retained some ground even in later times, also. The rulers of Sarabhpuria dynasty held sway in the region around Raipur during the 6th century A.D. They, however, had to shift to Orissa due to the advent of Panduvamsis of Dakshina Koshala. They were matrimonially linked with Magadha. Vasata, a princess of Magadha was married into this royal family of Sirpur. Excavations conducted in this capital city of Pandavas, has yielded large number of Buddhist remains assignable up to the 9th century A.D. The Kalchuris also held sway in this region during which many Brahmanical temples were constructed (Shukla 1994: 109-112, Vajpayee 1994: 113-118). Sullerey (1978: 113) comments on the lack of even a single Buddhist sculpture during the reign of the Kalchuris. Pertinently, according to him the popularity of Buddhism was on decline during this period. Other scholars tell of continuity of Buddhist activities during the rule of Kalchuris also (Dwivedi 1994:34; Tripathi and Mishra 1994: 136). However, in general it appears that Buddhist remains ascribable to this period are lesser in number. The fact also hints towards the need to explore Buddhist remains even more thoroughly. If conspicuous number of sites and remains are not found, then it can be safely surmised that Buddhism had reached its nadir in this region even before the heydays of Kalchuri rule.

Buddhist Remains

In the northern most district of Chhattisgarh, Ambikapur [Sarguja] there are several sites with Buddhist archaeological remains. These include, Kabir Chaura, and Jogi Mara in Ramgadh Hills. At the place known as Kabirchaura in Ramgarh hill has a votive stupa which is 'an object of worship among the aborginal tribes' (Verma 1989:292). Verma further mentions about a cave known as Jogi Mara with patches of painting that are similar to carvings of Sanchi and Bharhut. Evidently, these remains would be of comparable antiquity, if not earlier than the two latter mentioned sites (Verma 1989: 293,294). Sanna is a village about 51 km northwest of Jashpurnagar, which apparently has some Buddhist remains. Guru (1976:379) reports that in this village 'the idol installed in a temple strangely enough resembles that of the Buddha.

In Janjgir Distt. a village known as Kharod, has yielded a large number of Brahmanical sculptural and architectural remains but on the analogical basis of Buddhist statues kept in the brick temple at Seorinarayan nearby, Shrivastava (1978: 512) surmises that Buddhism thrived in this area and 'that some of the pillars may be of Buddhist origin'. A black stone sculpture having 'striking similarity with the Buddha image at Rajim has been reported from Seorinarayan (Shrivastava 1978: 524). The temple incidentally belongs to the Kalchuri period.

In Bilaspur district situated in the north western part of the state and bordering Madhya Pradesh, there are several Buddhist sites including Malhar. Malhar is situated on the ancient trade route (Thakur 1996:79). According to Tripathi and Mishra (1994:134-136) besides architectural remains, in the course of the excavations sculptures and other Buddhist artifacts including seals were obtained most of which belonged to the time period between 300-900 A.D. In general, however the presence of Buddhism in Malhar is apparent from 1st-2nd century AD to 10th century A.D. Besides other remains there are other stray sculptures like the bust of Buddha in ASI sculpture shed and yet another of Buddha in *bhumisparsha mudra* kept in the house of Shri Sudha Ram Gupta (Nagarch 1994: 39-44). The latter mentioned sculpture is dated to 6th cent A.D. Excavations done in the mid seventies have yielded a 'number of Buddhist sculptures'at the site (IAR 1974-75:21,22). A Buddhist Temple Complex enshrining an image of the *Vajrayana* Buddhism and three rooms for the monks were also reported from Malhar. According to the excavators 'a thick ashy deposit would perhaps indicate the destruction of the site by the Kalchuris'(IAR 1975-76: 23). Earlier, an inscribed image of Boddhisattva was reported at Nandur Khurd from the same district (IAR 1958-59 : 72) The inscription is ascribable to 8th-9th century A.D. From Gudikhar, temple and sculptural remains of *Vajrayan* Buddhism has been reported (IAR 1973-74:18,19).

South of Janjgir Distt. and south east of Bilaspur Distt. lies the capital of Chhattisgarh, Raipur. Rajim, located about 49 km towards south east of Raipur is a better known place, with reporting about the site from as early as the later part of 19th century. Considering the antiquity of the inscriptions, some of which are in shell characters, the site, evidently is very old and was pre eminent during its hey days. During his surveys Beglar (1878:148-154) had reported a cluster of several temples with a space enclosed by high walls. He was of the opinion that some of the temples here are of later construction, using materials of earlier temples. According to Rajendra Verma (1973: 560) "Rajim was seat of Buddhism (Fig. 1) and the Buddhist remains are used in the temple when Buddhism declined in the region." Further, according to Beglar (1878:151), the said representation of Rama in his form of Raja Lochana in the Rajib Lochana temple is in fact a Buddhist statue. Cunningham (reprint 1969:6-20) in the early part of 1880's had mentioned about a black stone statue of Buddha in one of the two corners of the inner chamber containing sculptures. According to him the sculpture is not in its original position even if it is thought as Buddha *Avatara* of Vishnu. Earlier, Beglar had stressed on other aspects including the presence of Buddhist rails. Not far from Raipur about 24 km south east of the city a village known as Reewa, reputedly have three mounds of Buddhist origin (Verma 1973: 563). Arang is nearly 34 km from Raipur on the national highway leading to Sambalpur.An image of Buddha in *bhumi sparsha mudra* with an inscription ascribable to the end of the eighth century A.D. has been reported from Arang (IAR 1968-69:65). The district Durg with its headquarter of the same name lies west of Raipur district. Broken images of Buddha have been reported from Durg (Sharma 1974: 268). Interestingly,'stone foot stools resembling Buddhist sculptures' were also found from the same town(Verma 1972: 447).

The district Mahasamund has two well-known sites with Buddhist remains. The sites, Sirpur and Turturiya, incidentaly, were known from the later part of the nineteenth century. During the earlier surveys, however nothing much about Buddhist remains were known from Sirpur. Beglar (1878 : 168-193) found a sculpture of Buddhist affinity amidst other sculptures stuck irregularly on a wall. Cunningham (reprint 1969 : 31) reported a colossal head of Buddha, 18 inches high near a broken temple at Chota kila, near Sirpur. On the basis of the large head he did surmise, without any other remains known then, that Buddhism was flourishing in Sirpur. He also asserted, that "Buddhism was eventually suppressed, and, perhaps, carefully rooted out by the utter ruin of all its temples and statues." Between the years 1953-1956 Dr. M.G. Dikshit conducted excavations (Sharma 2002 : 805) and reported large number of Buddhist architectural and sculptural remains. Two Buddhist temple and monastery complexes, namely Swastika Vihar and Anand Prabhu Vihar were exposed. Buddhist monastery and temple complexes are dated to the 7th to 9th century A.D. Both the complexes have cells around a central courtyard and contain large-sized images of the Buddha in *bhumi sparsha-mudra*, seated on high pedestals with the usual attendants (Dikshit 1960 : 21). According to Moreshwar G. Dikshit (1960 : 21) 'after the Pandavas, the Buddhist monasteries at

Sirpur were occupied by the people of the Saiva faith, who beheaded many of the Buddhist images and perhaps spared others because by that time the Buddha was already regarded as an *avatara* by the Hindu fold'. 'The Saivite intrusion in these monasteries was indicated by the discovery of crude plaques of Ganesa, Mahishamardini, Śiva-Parvti, etc.' (IAR 1954-55: 26). Recently, near Food Godown in the proximity of Laxman Temple Road on the basis of the broken pillars, sculptures including an image of Buddha the extant mound named as SRP-1 was excavated under the direction of A. K. Sharma. and J.P. Joshi. In the course of the excavations, a Buddhist Temple-cum-nunnery was exposed (Sharma 2002: 807-809). The excavations done here yielded besides image of Buddha in *bhumi-sparsha mudra* (Fig. 2), images of Manjushri and Avalokiteshwara. Stone drains from *garbgrihas* indicate that washing of the Buddha and Boddhisattvas with water had come to vogue. The site has yielded a number of badly damaged Buddhist sculptures (Joshi and Sharma 2000: 116 and IAR 1999-2000: 98). Although two coins dated to the Sultanate period have been recovered from the upper level of the site (IAR 1999-2000: 97-99), it appears that the site was abandoned much earlier since Kalchuri period remains is conspicuous by their absence at this site. Gandeshwar Temple in Sirpur was built of architectural members collected from the surrounding areas. Among other sculptures seen in this Shiv Temple two large Buddhist sculptures (Sharma 1994: 126-131) are particularly important. Buddhist sculptures of Sirpur have found place, especially in museums (Fig. 3) and also in sculpture sheds (Fig. 4), presumably in private collections, besides in temples of other affiliations and a full account is not known.

Turturiya is yet another site in this district, which according to Beglar (reprint 1970:147) has 'numerous Buddhist remains in the place'. At this site a brick stupa existed on the shoulder of the hill, much of which had slipped into the valley below, and also quarried away by the local residents when Beglar reported nearly 130 years before now. Among other things reported by him Buddha in the *dharma chakra pravartana mudra*, Padmapani besides others, and Buddhist formula inscribed pedestal dated to about ninth century A.D., deserve mention. Curiously, some of the lingams appear to have been evidently 'manufactured out of the smaller pillars of the Buddhist temples that once adorned the place' (Beglar reprint 1970 : 148; Verma 1973: 572, 573). Recently, Mohan Sahu a research scholar, visited the site and confirmed the existence of ornamentation in lower few inches of the Śiva linga and mentions that it has since been covered with freshly laid tiles (personal communication).

Dwivedi (1994 : 34, 36) mentions about a good number of Buddhist images observed at Deepadih, Silipacharahi and Gandai.

Chhattisgarh is not bereft of Buddhist remains in the southern part also. The best known site in this region is Bhongapal, which is situated about 30 km from Narayanpur and more than 300 km away from Raipur. The site proper is located nearly 3 km away from Bhongapal. Here the east facing brick built apsidal temple is constructed on a platform of about 1.70 m height. N.K. Pathak (1997:569) mentions the presence of a Buddha figure in the *bhusparsha mudra*-with both hands broken- in the sanctum of the apsidal temple.He has given a date of 6th century A.D. to this figure based on the opinion of V.D. Jha. There are some rectangular cells around the apsidal temple on the platform excluding the eastern side. Besides Bhongapal, Gobrahin and Jaityagiri are two other sites where Buddhist remains have been found hinting to the spread of Buddhism in Gupta period or at least in the post Gupta period (Tripathi and Mishra 1994 : 133). Burnt brick stupas of the Gupta period have been reported from Gobrahin (IAR 1984-85:40). Stupa has been reported also at Gadh Dhanora in Bastar (Dikshit 1994:34)

Discussion

Evidently, the cornucopia of Buddhist remains is much more than the sites briefly touched upon herein. These have to be searched-perhaps-intensively and subjectively initially, to overcome the fogging effects of ravages of nature and man. Once each site or sculpture is seen through the perspective of its possibility of having Buddhist affiliation, then each could be ascribed, on objective analysis, their actual respective affiliations. Dwivedi (1994:34-36) did identify Buddhist sculptures earlier identified as merely *dwarpalas.* The Bhandak stone record of Pandava ruler Nannadeva mentions of restoration of a Buddhist temple built by an ancient king (Agrawala 1994: 69) As the place is not mentioned as such the site could not be pinpointed without element of doubt. Guru (1976a : 22), however has mooted that the site where the temple was conserved is Arang. On the other hand, at sites like Turturiya reexplorations and systematic excavations have to be carried out such that a fair idea about the total impact of Buddhism in its heydays could be gauged. As Jha (1994: 10) in the context of Sarguja Distt.says 'though place names like Saramana (Sramana) Sirimathakhoh (named after Sirimata Deota) and Buddha Sagara clearly indicate the Buddhist influence, the Buddhist icons are conspicuous by their absence'. Moreover, some scholars can only give cognizance to patronage given to Buddhism but deny vehemently the universal phenomenon of religious strife that also occurred in the subcontinent even before the invasions from West Asia.

Conclusion

Given the evidence of trade routes passing through the region and of the religion existing from about 2nd century B.C., over 20 Buddhist sites reported is only a natural corollary. Many of the sites have yielded a variety of finds in large quantity and outstanding quality which goes to show that Chhattisgarh was a strong hold of Buddhism in the few centuries around the middle of the first millennium A.D. However, there is a need for extensive surveys and a resurvey of the earlier known sites, making an elaborate inventory of these sites, conduct excavations wherever clarity of religious affiliation and the sequence of historical phases of the sites are not known. Even a closer scrutiny of sculptures in museums, sculpture sheds, abandoned temples and those in worship should be done. All these would enable the realistic assessment of the full impact of Buddhism, its rise and fall and the socio-political reasons, thereof.

Acknowledgements

I am thankful to Smt Hemlata Ukhale, Librarian, Archaeological Survey of India, Bhopal circle for providing all relevant literature at the earliest, to Shri R Movendran, Assistant Archaeologist, for providing photographs and to Vijay Mishra for rendering technical assistance.

REFERENCES

Agrawala, P.K. 1994 *Some Epigraphical Notes on Early Art of Chhattisgarh*, Puratan 9, p. 69

Ahmed, N. 1994 *The Attribution of the Repouse Gold Coins of Mahendraditya and Kumaragupta : A Review*, Puratan 9, p.55.

Beglar, J.D. 1878 *Report of a tour in Bundelkhand and Malwa 1871-72 and in the Central Provinces 1873-74*, Office of the Superintendent of Govt. Printing. Calcutta pp. 148-154,159-165, 168-193, 196-201.

Beglar, J.D. 1970 (reprint) *Report of Tours in the South-Eastern Provinces in 1874-75 and 1875-76*. Office of the Superintendent of Govt. Printing, Calcutta, pp. 147, 148.

Cunningham, A. 1969 (reprint) *Report of a Tour in the Central*

		Provinces and Lower Gangetic Doab in 1881-82, Indological Book House, Delhi, pp. 6-31
Dikshit, M.G.	1960	*Sirpur and Rajim Temples,* N.M. Tripathi Private Ltd., Bombay, pp. 14-23, 26-32.
Dikshit, R.	1994	*Naga Shasankalin Bastar Ki Dharmik Awastha,* Journal of the Madhya Pradesh Itihasa Parishad No. 16, p. 34.
Dwivedi, S.K.	1994	*The Dwarpala images in Khairagadh Museum—An Observation,* Puratan-9, pp. 34-38.
Guru, S.D.	1976	*RaigarhDistrict Gazetteer*, Bhopal, p. 379.
Guru, S.D.	1976a.	*Buddhism in Dakshina Kosala*, Journal of the Madhya Pradesh Itihas Parishad No. 10, p. 22.
Indian Archaeology	1954-55	A Review, p. 26
Indian Archaeology	1958-59	A Review, p. 72
Indian Archaeology	1968-69	A Review, p. 65
Indian Archaeology	1973-74	A Review, pp. 18,19
Indian Archaeology	1974-75	A Review, pp. 21-22
Indian Archaeology	1975-76	A Review, pp. 23
Indian Archaeology	1984-85	A Review, p. 40.
Indian Archaeology	1996-97	A Review, pp. 65, 66.
Indian Archaeology	1999-00	A Review, pp. 97-99.
Jha, V.D.	1978	*Megalithic Monuments in Bastar*, Prachya Pratibha, Vol. VI, No. 2, pp. 61-65.
Jha, V.D.	1994	*The Art of Saraguja*, Puratan-9, pp. 10-16.
Mishra, P.K.	2000	*Deorkothar Stupa: New light on Early Buddhism,* Marg, Vol. 52, No. 1, pp. 69-74.
Joshi, J.P. and Sharma, A.K.	1999-2000	*Excavation at Sirpur, Distt Mahasamund, Chhattisgarh,* Puratattva 30, pp. 110-116.
Mitra, D.	2001	(Reprint) *Sanchi*, Archaeological Survey of

India, New Delhi, p. 16, Nagarch, B.L., 1994 *Patalesvara Mahadeva and Other Temples And Sculpture at Malhar,* Distt. Bilaspur (M.P.). Puratan-9, pp. 39-44.

Pandey, R.P. 1994 *Prehistoric Cultural Growth in Natural Perspectives in the Chhattisgarh Region, Central India,* Puratan-9, pp. 1-3.

Pathak, N.K. 1997 *Bhongapal Ka Nalyugin Boudh Chaityagriha Evam Mandir* (in Hindi) in K.K. Chakravarty and O.P. Mishra (Eds), *The Bounteous Tree:* Treasures in Indian Art and Culture, Sharda Publishing House, Delhi p. 569.

Sharma, M. 1994 *Sirpur Ki Prastar Buddha Pratimayein* (in Hindi) Puratan-9, pp. 126-131.

Sharma, R.K. 1974 *Madhya Pradesh Kay Puratattva Ka Sandarbha Grantha* (Hindi) Madhya Pradesh Hindi Granth Academy, Bhopal, p. 268.

Sharma, A.K. 2002 *Excavation at Mansar and Sirpur-Flash,* in Margabandhu, C., A.K. Sharma and R.S. Bisht (eds.) Puraratna, Agam Kala Prakashan, Delhi pp. 805-809.

Shrivastav, P.N. 1978 *Bilaspur District Gazetteer*, Bhopal, pp. 512, 515, 524.

Shukla, S. 1994 *Kalchuriyon Kay Mandir: Ek Drishtikon* (in Hindi) Puratan 9, pp. 109,112.

Sullerey, S.K. 1978 *Chhattisgarh Ki Kala ka Dharmik va Samajik Paksha* (in Hindi) Prachya Pratibha, Vol. VI, No. 1, p.113.

Thakur, V.K. 1996 *Urban Form in Transition: Archaeologically situating Gupta Towns of Madhya Pradesh in Indian History,* Prachya Pratibha, Vol. XVII, p. 79.

Tripathi, K.K. and O.P. Mishra 1994 D*akshin Koshal (Chhattisgarh) Kshetra May Boudh-Dharma* (in Hindi), Puratan-9, pp. 132-137.

Vajpayee, S.K.	1994	*Durg Jilay Kay Kalchurikalin Mandir* (in Hindi) Puratan-9, pp. 113-118.
Verma, R.	1972	*Durg District Gazetteer*, Bhopal, p. 447
Verma, R.	1973	*Raipur District Gazetteer*, Bhopal, pp. 560, 563, 572, 573
Verma, R.	1989	*Surguja District Gazetteer*, Bhopal, pp. 292-294.

13

CHALCOLITHIC CULTURE OF MIDDLE GANGA PLAIN: EMERGENCE OF AN EXPANDED VILLAGE SOCIETY

—*Kulbhushan Mishra*[1]

Introduction

The entire Ganga plain is divided into three units: (i) The Upper (ii) The Middle and (iii) The Lower. The middle Ganga plain (24°30'N-27°50'N and 81°47'E -87°50'E) covers a long physical area of 144,409 sq. km. This plain has its maximum length from the east to west is about 600 km while its width from north to south is approximately 330 km (Singh, R.L., 1971 : 183-84). The Middle Ganga plain extends from Ganga-Yamuna confluence in the west, Rajmahal hills in the east, the Himalayas in the north and Vindhyas in the south. The region is mainly drained by Ganga, though its regional drainage are the Ghaghara, Gandak, Kosi, Son and other tributaries (Singh, R.L., 1971 : 193).

The archaeological investigations carried out since the last fifty years have brought to light hundreds of Chalcolithic settlements spread over different parts of the country like Deccan, Central India, Rajasthan, Gujarat and Ganga Plain. All these settlements are marked by their characteristic features and determined by their respective ecological settings. The Chalcolithic culture of middle Ganga plain was preceded by the Neolithic culture of this region. There is no cultural gap at most of the sites in between Neolithic and Chalcolithic period. The Introduction of Copper/ Bronze tools, though limited quantity of stone tools continued to be used

---

1. Indian Archaeological Society.

side by side during the Chalcolithic period. This stage witnessed a marked increase in the number of settlements, introduction of copper-bronze for the manufacture of tools, weapons and ornaments, and also a distinct improvement in architecture. In the present paper the author proposes to look into the various issues of cultural development of this region. The study is based on the data obtained through excavations of Chalcolithic sites in Middle Ganga Plain.

EXCAVATED CHALCOLITHIC SITES OF MIDDLE GANGA PLAIN

Sohagaura (Lat. 26^{0}32"N, Long. 80^{0}32"E)

It is situated on the confluence of river Rapti and Ami in Gorakhpur district. Excavation here was conducted by G.C. Pande on behalf of the Department of Ancient Indian History, Culture and Archaeology, Gorakhpur University in 1961-62 and re-excavated by S.N. Chaturvedi in 1974-75 (IAR 1961-62: 56; 1974-75: 46-47). The total habitational deposits has revealed six cultural periods, from Neolithic to Medieval period. Period II and III was marked by the Chalcolithic culture. The associated pottery of this period include black-and-red ware, black-slipped ware, burnished grey and red wares. Besides these the earlier tradition of corded and rusticated wares continued (Chaturvedi 1985 : 104).

Chirand: (Lat. 25^{0}45'N; Long. 84^{0}50'E)

The site is situated in district Saran in Bihar, and was excavated by B.P.Sinha and V.S.Verma for seven seasons from 1962-63 to 1972-73 (IAR 1962-63:6-8; 1968-69: 5-6; 1969-70:3-4; 1970-71: 6-7; 1971-72: 6-7). The total habitation is divided into five fold cultural periods, from Neolithic to Late Historical. Period II represents the Chalcolithic culture and distinct potteries are black and red ware, black slipped ware, both plain and painted. The main types of BRW include: dish-on-stand, long necked jar, slipped bowl, basin, bowl with ring base, spouted vessel etc. A few sherds of the black ware show white painting.

Koldihwa: (Lat.24^{0}54'N; Long. 82^{0}2'E)

Koldihwa is located in district Allahabad on the left bank of the river Belan in Meja Tahsil. The site was excavated by the Allahabad University under the direction of G.R.Sharma, D. Mandal and J.N. Pal from 1973-74 to 1975-76 (IAR 1973-74: 26-27; 1975-76: 46-47). The excavation has revealed a culture sequence from Neolithic to early phase of Iron Age. Period II was characterized by Chalcolithic culture and associated pottery was wheel thrown, made of well levigated clay which comprise of red ware (both plain and slipped) black-slipped ware, black and red ware.

Khairadih: (Lat. 26⁰10'N; Long. 83⁰51'30"E)

The site is located in Balia district of Uttar Pradesh and is situated on the right bank of river Ghagra. It was excavated by the Banaras Hindu University under the joint direction of Prof. K.K. Sinha and B.P. Singh in five seasons from 1980-81 to 83-84 and 85-86 (Singh, B.P. 1988:28). The excavation has provided three successive cultural periods. Period I is Pre-NBP deposits and characterized by BRW, black slipped ware (both plain and painted), red ware consisting of both slipped and un-slipped and limited number of them are painted as well. Period II is marked by the emergence of NBPW and period III is characterized by red ware.

Narhan: (Lat. 26⁰19'N; Long. 83⁰24'E)

It is located on the left bank of river Ghaghara in Gola tehsil of district Gorakhpur. The site was excavated by Purushottam Singh in 1983-84 to 87-88. Excavation has brought to light a five-fold culture sequence. Period I is termed as Narhan culture (Singh,P.1994:9-15) and is characterized by a white painted black and red ware, black slipped ware, sometimes bearing white paintings, a red slipped ware and plain red ware, the black and red ware represented by bowls, basins and vases, but dishes are absent.

Senuwar: (Lat. 24⁰56'N; Long. 83⁰56'E)

The site of Senuwar is located in district Rohtas in Bihar. It was excavated by B.P. Singh in 1986-87 and 1989-90 have brought to light significant evidence for the development of Neolithic into the Chalcolithic phases through an intermediary stage of the Neolithic-Chalcolithic. The four fold culture division of Senuwar comprised of period I Neolithic, II Chalcolithic, III NBW-culture and period IV belongd to Kushana phase (Singh,B.P.1996:75). In Chalcolithic period all the basic traits of Neolithic culture continued in spite of the fact that metal technology was introduced. Besides the continuation of earlier ceramics e.g., cord impressed, rusticated, burnished grey and BRW, main ceramics of this period are the BRW, BSW, red ware, and burnished black ware (these are all both plain and painted).

Imlidih Khurd: (Lat. 26⁰30'30"N; Long. 83⁰12'5"E)

It is located about half kilometer north west of Sikariganj town on the Gorakhpur Gola road. It was excavated by Purushottam Singh in 1992 and 1993. Excavation has brought to light a three-fold cultural sequence. Period II is Narhan culture and marked by intense structural activity comprising of two successive mud floors having several post holes and ovens. The main ceramics include coarse black and red ware, black slipped ware and plain red ware (Singh, P. 1993: 31-32)

Jhusi: (Lat. 25⁰26'10"N; Long. 81⁰54'30"E)

The site is situated about 7 km. east of Allahabad city and located on the left bank of river Ganga, very close to the Ganga-Yamuna confluence. The ancient name of the site was Pratisthanpur. Excavation was conducted by V.D. Misra and his team in 1995. Excavation has yielded a five fold cultural periods. Period I belongs to Chalcolithic culture (Misra, V.D. et al 1996: 63-64) which is characterized by black slipped ware, black burnished ware, red ware and black and red ware.

Malhar: Lat. (24⁰59'16"N; Long. 83⁰15'46"E)

The site is situated on left bank of Karmnasa river in Chakia tahsil of district Chandauli, south Uttar Pradesh. It was excavated by Rakesh Tewari in 1999. Excavation has revealed a four-fold cultural sequence. Period I belongs to pre-iron phase and ceramics include red ware, black and red ware, (both plain and painted) and black ware (Tewari, R. et all 2000: 69-70).

Raja Nal Ka Tila: (Lat.83⁰18'41"& 83⁰19'26"N; Long. 24⁰42'5"& 24⁰41'51"E)

The site is situated in district Sonbhadra. It was excavated by the department of U.P. State Archaeology, under the general supervision of Rakesh Tewari in 1995-96 (Tewari, R. 1997: 77-78). The total cultural deposits were divided into three periods. Period I is represented BRW, red ware, BSW, grey ware and black ware. The main shapes include bowls and water vessels, storage jars and few miniature pots.

Agiabir: (Lat. 25⁰13'52"N; Long. 82⁰38'41"E)

The settlement is situated on the left bank of river Ganga, in district Mirzapur of eastern Uttar Pradesh. Site was excavated by the Banaras Hindu University under the direction of Purushottam Singh and Ashok Kumar Singh, for three field seasons between 1999 to 2001. The excavation resulted into five-fold cultural sequence. Period I is Narhan culture and marked by the presence of BRW, BSW and red ware. BRW and BSW bear linear painting in white. The main types of BRW are bowl, storage jars, lipped basins, and dish on stands (Singh and Singh 2000: 31-32).

Tokwa: (Lat. 24⁰54'20"N; Long. 82⁰16'45"E)

The site is situated on the confluence of the Belan and Adwa River in Mirzapur district of Uttar Pradesh. It is excavated by the Department of Ancient India History Culture and Archaeology, Allahabad University Under the guidance of V.D. Misra and his team in 2000. The combined testimonies of the excavation have evidence of three cultures: I Neolithic II Chalcolithic III Iron Age. The associated potteries of Chalcolithic culture are black and red ware, BSW, and red ware. Characteristic pottery types include different types of bowls, dishes, basins, footed and perforated basins, medium sized vases, store jars and pedestal bowls (Misra. V.D, et al. 2001: 59-63)

Lahuradeva: (Lat. 26°46'N; Long. 82°57'E)

The site is situated in district Sant Kabir Nagar in Uttar Pradesh. It has been excavated by Rakesh Tewari in 2001-2002 to 2005-2006. After the first season's excavation the total deposits are divided into five-folds cultural periods. Pd I early farming phase (Sub-period A, Sub-period B), Period II developed farming phase (Chalcolithic culture), period III advanced farming phase (early Iron age), period IV NBPW phase, period V Early Historic (Tewari et al. 2002:54-56).Period II with a deposit of maximum 1.60 m and is marked by the appearance of painted and plain black slipped ware. Other ceramics include red ware, BRW (both plain and painted) black and grey wares. The shapes include dish-on-stands, bowl-on-stands, pedestal bowls, perforated legged vessel, lipped vessel, disc based bowl, spouted and convex sided dishes etc.

Other excavated Chalcolithic sites of this region such as Dhuriapar (Singh1992), Waina (Singh & Singh 1996), Bhunadih (Singh1998), Prahladpur (IAR1962-63), Saraimohana (IAR 1967-68), Kamauli (IAR 1963-64), Masondih (IAR 1964-65), Aktha (Jaiswal, V.2002) in Uttar Pradesh and Manghi (IAR 1983-84), Maner (IAR 1984-85), Oriup (IAR 1966-67), Champa (IAR 1974-75), Checher Kutubpur (IAR 1977-78) Sonepur (IAR 1970-71) in Bihar have further supplemented the material culture and life ways of Chalcolithic people in middle Ganga plain.

Chronology:

For the chronology of the Chalcolithic culture in MGP, the radio carbon dates have been obtained from the sites i.e. Sohagaura 1230±130 B.C. and 1330 ± 110 B.C. (Possehl and Rissman 1992: 463), Narhan cal. 1380± 110 and cal. 1390 ± 110 B.C. (Singh 1994: 32). Chirand has yielded five dates ranging between 715±105 B.C. to 1650±100 B.C. (Agrawal D.P. 1984: 279). Khairadih has three dates 950±150 B.C., 1030±160 B.C., 3070 ± 90 BP (B.P. Singh. 1988: 33).Lahuradeva period II cal. 1399 B.C. and cal. 1750 B.C. (Tewari et al. 2005-6: 73). Koldihwa have two dates—1450±120 B.C. and 1035±155 B.C. (Possehl and Rissman 1992: 461). Malhar is placed between 1950 B.C. to 1700-1600 B.C. (Tewari R. et al. 2000: 88). Rajanal Ka Tila have time bracket from 1700 to 1300 B.C (Tewari R.

2000: 93). Senuwar period II transition phase between Neolithic/Chalcolithic have datable in c. 1950 B.C. to 1300 B.C and period III Chalcolithic have placed in c. 1300 B.C. to 7th -6th century B.C. (Singh B.P.2001: 111-113).

The combined analysis of Archaeological data and given C^{14} dates, of the Chalcolithic culture of middle Ganga plain would suggest a time bracket from 2nd millennium B.C to the 9th-8th century B.C. or later.

Structural Remains:

The inhabitants of Chalcolithic period lived in wattle and daub houses, fragment of burnt clay with red marks and patched of floors and post-holes have been recorded from all the sites in this region. Screens of the walls of these hutments were plastered with mud on both the sides. Excavation at Lahuradeva have also furnished evidence of post holes, burnt clay nodules often bearing reed marks, hearths. Among these the most remarkable evidence is seen in the construction of earthen storage bins or silos. Other sites like Tokwa, Agiabir, Raja Nal Ka Tila, Senuwar, Jhusi etc. have similar type of evidences. Occurrence of bins or silos, *kothilas* and baked/unbaked oval or cylindrical mud bases suggested the existence of grains storage.

Faunal remains:

Faunal remains of domesticated and wild variety have been reported from the excavated sites in this region. Domesticated variety include cattle, buffalo, sheep, goat, pig and dog and wild animals include deer, nilgai, sambar, antelope, gazelle, and wild pig. Besides these, remains of birds and aquatic creatures like fish and tortoise have also been found.

Botanical remains:

A good quality of archaeo-botanical remains have been reported from several sites of MGP. Cultivated cereals included three type of wheat ș club wheat, bread wheat and dwarf wheat; Cultivated rice (*Oryza sativa*), Italian millet, jowar millet, Ragi millet, kodon millet, green gram (*Mung*) and *Khesari* etc. Mustard oilseeds found from Narhan in period I is the first record of this species from Indian sub continent. Seeds of Jackfruit found from this level show another important discovery. Besides this evidence of mango and grape seeds, date, *nux vomica* and *tulasi* are also found. All these evidence shows that the agricultural practices were quite advanced.

Cultural Assemblage:

The Chalcolithic people in Middle Ganga plain used a large variety of objects including bone tools, microliths, metal objects, beads, terracotta objects etc.

Microliths consisting of cores, flakes and finished tools-parallel sided blades, blunted back blades, serrated blades, points, lunates, arrowheads, scrapers, tri-angles and trapezes etc. All these are fashioned on semiprecious stone like chalce-dony, chert, agate, carnelian and quartz etc. At Chalcolithic level of Agiabir (district Mirzapur U.P) Microliths including blades, cores, bladelets, retouches and flakes have been found. In the site of Chirand, at Sonepur and Oriu have also been found microliths of similar kind.

Metal Objects:

The occurrence of copper objects though limited in number, comprise knives, spearheads and arrowheads. An important finding from Khairadih is a socketed arrow head having two perforations on the socket (Singh, B.P., 1988:32). A bead from Koldihwa and an antimony rod from Chirand have been reported. At Lahuradeva copper objects are known in small quantity. These include fishing hook, antimony rod, and nail cutter (Tewari et al 2002: 56). Agiabir and Imlidih Khurd have yielded copper objects of only fishing hook. Besides these, there are sites like Koldihwa, Rajanal Ka Tila, Malhar, Narhan and Chirand etc. which have also yielded iron objects. These iron objects though limited in quantity appears in the mid phase of Chalcolithic period at most of these sites (Tripathi. V, 2006: 110-111). Above all these evidences reflect that all along there is a peculiar scarcity of metal seen in Chalcolithic period of middle Ganga plain.

Ornaments:

Chalcolithic people used variety of ornaments like beads, pendants, bangles, rings and ear-studs. The evidence has been recovered from many sites such as Sohgaura, Imlidih-khurd, Chirand, Checher Kutbpur, Lahuradeva, Senuwar and Agiabir. Beads made of semi precious stones, and occasionally of bone, conch-shell, faince, steatite and copper have also been reported. Agate was the most favoured material and the presence of unfinished beads of this stone right in Chalcolithic period demonstrate that it was locally manufactured. These are in different shapes like cylindrical, barrel, rectangular, and conical, ghat shaped, pear shaped etc. Terracotta beads have also been reported in all the sites.

Bone Tools:

It is a most important feature and an essential cultural component of Chalcolithic period in middle Ganga plain. The tools made of cut bones and antler consists of a variety of arrow heads, socketed, barbed and tanged, and other types like chisels, adzes, dagger, awls, scrapers and points etc. Some of the polished and decorated bone arrow-heads found from Lahuradewa show fine workmanship. Excavation at Senuwar also has yielded a variety of tools ș double ended point, barbed and socketed arrow-head, borer and scraper cum point.

Ceramic Industry:

The main ceramic industry of this period are BRW, red ware, BSW, RSW, and grey ware. The pottery is largely wheel turned, made of well levigated clay and sometimes tempering material has also been used. BRW, BSW, Coarse red ware, red slipped ware burnished black ware (these are plain and painted). Corded and restricted wares have also been reported but they seen to be an element of survival of nelolithic traditions. These wares are reported in the corresponding levels from most of the sites such as Sohagaura, Imlidih khurd, Narhan, Khairadih, Agiabir and Lahuradewa etc. in middle Ganga plain.

The common shapes of this reign are bowls, dishes, basins, various sizes of jars, funnel-shaped lids. Bowls of various types include ș shallow, straight or convex sided, carinated, lipped and channel. BRW is represented in a variety of shapes—bowl, dish, lipped and plain basins and dish on stands. The painting motif shows a vertical or horizontal lines slanting lines, dots etc.

The types included in BSW are vases and small and medium size pots, bowl, basins, and funnel. However the types of Red ware comprise bowls, basin, beaker, button-based goblets and funnel-shaped lids. Medium size vases, show storage jars, shallow dishes, footed and perforated vessels. Designs executed include—wavy lines, vertical and horizontal bands, criss ș crosses, floral designs etc.

Detailed analysis of the ceramics of middle Ganga Chalcolithic reveal many significant features of their material culture. These may be serialized below:

1. The firing technique and thin fabric of many of the pot sherds indicate that the potters of this region were well advanced in their knowledge of pot making. Availability of plenty of wood for firing these pots show a large population density. Cutting of wood and transporting them to the site is extremely labour intensive and hence one has to accept a reasonably well organized social structure existing in these settlements.

2. The occurrence of dish and bowl on hollow stands is rather enigmatic. A population largely inhabiting in mud floored wattle-and-daub structures may find it difficult to use these objects on stands. At the same time the fact that they were made in good number shows the possibility of the existence of a power polarity which would indicate the development of a group of individuals as belonging to an elite class.

Conclusion

With the respect forestation in Ganga Plain, Rakesh Tewari. He says that "The Middle Ganga Plain and Himalayan *Tarai* had no forest cover of relatively greater density" (Tewari, R. 2004:12). The agricultural evidences obtained from various sites in this region clearly proved that enough land was available for agriculture in the surrounding area of the sites. All the major crops including rice, wheat, millets and pulses were being cultivated in sufficient quantities. Because of that, Chalcolithic inhabitants produced enough food without much help of metal implements. This favourable condition appears to be responsible for an increase in population and settlements of this period. The foregoing account of material remains from Neolithic to NBPW levels shows a gradual and continuous development of culture.

One would like to ask at this juncture, why the material culture evidence from the region do not show any indication of a rise of a state like what has been observed in the north-west and western part of India. Varieties of opinion have been expressed about why a state emerges at one place and why no such phenomenon is observed in another place. All these opinions cluster around economic factors. For the middle Ganga region it will appear that the economy could not have been bad at all. One can see this from the mushrooming of these Chalcolithic settlements all over this region. V.D. Misra while describing the Food production and settlement pattern in MGP (Misra, 2007:144-145), has also pointed out the absence of urbanization in the Chalcolithic phase.

After a close look at the content, environment and material culture of these sites one can arrive at some important factors which prevented the region from developing a complex settlement similar to the one seen at a statehood culture.

The statehood need not emerge on the basis of surplus of subsistence unless the social structure develops a strong polarity of political power. This enables the leader to manipulate the surplus for constructing public buildings etc. Thus, Ganga valley would appear as a colonization of villages adapted to fishing and hunting for their protein intake. In addition to the agriculture is low land and small clearing must have provided a reasonable subsistence. The villages may have been linked by extended kinship linkage and conflict resolution might have been done through gathering and feasting. These gatherings are always given a religious rider in the form of ancestor worship of the lineage head. This social system is self operating and does not require any outside monitoring. Such a system is in sharp contrast to the concept of a state where conflict resolution needs to be done on the basis of a set of rules laid down by the head of the stratified system.

If Middle Ganga Chalcolithic did not care to develop a state it is possibly because the intensification of subsistence by cutting forest was very difficult in this ecology. The relatively forested region with multiple rivers rendered these areas infested with wild animals. Consequently the mindset remained organized to develop an advanced village structure at the most from a simple village but never a state.

BIBLIOGRAPHY

Agarwal, D.P. 1984. Archaeology of India, New Delhi.

Chaturvedi, S.N. 1985. Advance of Vindhyan Neolithic and Chalcolithic Cultures to the Himalayan Tarai: Excavation and Exploration in the Sarayaupar Region of Uttar Pradesh, *Man and Environment* IX: 101-108.

Indian Archaeology: A Review 1961-62.

Indian Archaeology: A Review 1962-63.

Indian Archaeology: A Review 1963-64.

Indian Archaeology: A Review 1964-65.

Indian Archaeology: A Review 1966-67.

Indian Archaeology: A Review 1967-68.

Indian Archaeology: A Review 1970-71.

Indian Archaeology: A Review 1973-74.

Indian Archaeology: A Review 1974-75.

Indian Archaeology: A Review 1975-76.

Indian Archaeology: A Review 1977-78.

Indian Archaeology: A Review 1983-84.

Indian Archaeology: A Review 1984-85.

Jayaswal, V., 2002. Aktha; A Satellite Settlement at Sarnath, Varanasi, *Bharti,* Vol. 26, Bulletin of the department of Ancient Indian History Culture and Archaeology, BHU: 61-80 .

Misra, V.D, B.B. Mishra, J.N. Pandey, J.N. Pal. 1996. A Preliminary Report of Excavation at Jhusi, 1995. *Pragdhara* 6: 63-66.

Misra,V.D, J.N. Pal, M.C. Gupta 2001. Excavation at Tokwa: A Neolithic-Chalcolithic Settlement, *Pragdhara* 11:59-72.

Misra,V.D. 2007. Food Production and Settlment ṣ Transition from Neolithic to the Chalcolithic: The Indian Scene, History of Science, Philosophy and Culture in Indian Civilization; Vol. 1, Part 4, G.C. Pande (ed), Centre for Studies in Civilization: 132-149.

Possehl, G.L. and Paul Rissman 1992. Chronology in the Old World Archaeology, (India) Vol. 1, IIIrd Edition, R.W. Ehrich (ed), University of Chicago Press/ Chicago and London.

Singh, R.L. (ed) 1971. *India : A Regional Geography,* National Geographic Society of India, Varanasi.

Singh, B.P. 1988. Khairadih—A Chalcolithic Settlement.*Puratattva* 18: 28-34.

Singh, P. 1994. Excavation at Narhan (1984-89) Delhi & Varanasi: BHU & B.R. Corporation.

Singh, B.P. 1996. Transformation of Cultures in Middle Ganga Plains: A Case Study of Senuwar, *Pragdhara* 6: 75-93.

Singh, P. 1993. Archaeological Excavation at Imlidih khurd 1992. *Pragdhara* 3: 21-35

Singh, P., A.K. Singh and I. Singh 1992. Trial Digging at Dhuriapar, *Pragdhara* 2: 55-60.

Singh, P. and A.K. Singh 1996. Excavation at Waina, District Balia, (U.P.) *Pragdhara* 6: 41-61.

Singh, P. and A.K. Singh 1998. Excavation at Bhunadih, District Balia, (U.P.) *Pragdhara* 8: 11-29.

Singh, P. and A.K. Singh 2000. Excavation at Agiabir, District Mirzapur (Uttar Pradesh). *Pragdhara* 10: 31-55.

Tewari, R., R.K.Srivastava, K.S.Saraswat and K.K.Singh 2000. Excavtion at Malhar, District Chandauli (U.P.) 2000: A Preliminary Report. *Pragdhara* 10:69-98.

Tewari, R. and R.K. Sivastava 1997. Excavation at RAJA NALA KA TILA (1995-96), District Saonbhadra (U.P.). Preliminary Observation, *Pragdhara* 7: 77-95.

Tewari, R., R.K. Srivastava, K.K. Singh 2002. Excavation at Lahuradeva, District Sant Kabir Nagar, Uttar Pradesh. *Puratattva* 32: 54-59.

Tewari, R., R.K. Srivastava, K.K. Singh, K.S. Saraswat 2006. Further Excavation at Lahuradeva, District Sant Kabir Nagar (U.P.) 2005-06. Preliminary Observations, *Puratattva* 36: 68.75.

Tewari, R. 2004. The Myth of Dense Forests and Human Occupation in the Ganga Plain. *Man and Environment* XXIX (2): 102-116.

Singh, B.P. 2001. Stages of Culture development in the Middle Ganga Plain- A Case Study of Senuwar. *Pragdhara* 11: 109-118.

Tripathi, V. 2006. Iron Technology, its Impact and Survival in the Middle Ganga Plain. *Pragdhara* 16: 109-123.

14

NEELKANTH TEMPLE, KALINJAR FORT

—Mohan Chandra Joshi

Introduction :

In the past, it was not an easy task to reach Kalinjar fort frequently due to its remote location and not having proper approach. Besides, this area has been affected from crucial dacoit problem for a very long time. Despite that some of the enthusiastic scholars did a great job on Kalinjar fort and published valuable accounts. Kalinjar fort (Lat. 25°00? N. and Long. 80°29° E) is one of the most famous forts in India preserving its 2000 years of history. The fort stands on a high hill of Vindhyan range in tahsil Narayani of district Banda, U.P. (Fig.1). The area of Kalinjar fort is 1.45 square Kilometers. It has an elevation of 374.90 meter above the sea and some 213.36 meter above that of the surrounding ground level[1]. The fort area consists of various architectural styles, inscriptions, rock-cut reservoirs, rock-cut paintings, and a rich collection of sculptures of Saiva-cult. Kalinjar fort is said to have been constructed by the Chandellas but no inscription proclaims so. However, there are more than 100 inscriptions engraved on the walls, buildings, tanks, etc. in and outside the fort. The present work is an attempt to deal with the Neelkanth temple which is a popular pilgrimage site from ancient times. Previously, Cunningham[2] wrote about Neelkanth temple along with other structures of the fort. Besides, Virginia Fass[3], Dr. Sushil Kumar Sullere[4] have shown their interest in dealing with the Neelkanth temple.

Temple details :

The temple of Neelkanth (Pl. 1) presently the chief object of worship at Kalinjar fort has equally been popular for many centuries as many pilgrims' records indicate. The temple is located at the western side (Fig. 2) of the fort at the upper portion of the hill and bordered by triple surrounding wall from eastern and western side. To reach the temple from the fort side there are two gates on the high hill, the upper most named as Neelkanth gate. After descending about 30 steps another small gate has been constructed. From this gate, a long way of steps has to be covered up to reach the temple.

This west facing temple (Fig. 3) is comprised of a rock-cut *garbha-griha* and a pillared *mandapa* in front. The rock-cut *lingam* in the *garbha-griha* is facing north-west having height of 4.5 feet and carved out on a two tired low platform shown with *chandrasila* (Pl. 2). Fine mouldings are provided on the platform. Another *lingam* smaller in size is also carved out at the left side of main lingam. At south-western side a sculpture of Parvati is depicted.

Garbha-griha is having an octagonal plan with flat roof. The ceiling of the garbha-griha is highly weathered. In the rear, just in front of the entrance, at the right side of the lingam, a door opening (Pl. 3) measures 0.55 m on width and 1.45 m. in height has been provided which further leads a passage around the garbha-griha and might had been served as a *pradakshina patha*. This passage is now closed. The same kind of door opening is at the left side of the *lingam* which is also closed. There are some outstanding sculptures carved out on the rock in the passage but these are difficult to access. The door opening at right side possesses one human figure on either side at the base and an inscription on the left side pilaster. The female figure at the right side is in *tribhanga* posture. Both the legs, left and right hand and the face is chopped off. The figure is adorned with necklaces and decorated girdle. The left side human figure is completely chopped off. However, only left hand's upper part survives. The pilaster is decorated above the human figures with floral motifs. At the left side of the left pilaster, there is a figure of *keechakas*. The walls of the *garbha-griha* are decorated with human sculptures of devotees (Pl.4) depicted in the panels shown on the top of the wall along with ceiling. Ceiling of the *garbha-griha* is supported by two pillars (Pl. 5) at the front side. The right side pillar is measured 2.45m in height and 0 .30 m. wide at the base. The base of the pillar is square and comparatively higher and the central part is octagonal with conical cuts on the top. The upper part of the pillar is fine and circular with a circular capital on the top. An inscription is engraved at the square part at the base. The pillar at the left side consists of four parts. The base portion is square and two tired diminishing in size. Above this, a sculpted panel is shown. The sculptures are badly mutilated. Hardly male-figures' torso at the front side is visible. Above this portion an octagonal shaft with floral design is seen. The upper most part is shown with load bearers in octagonal semi-circular design. The height

Fig. 14.1. Location map of Kalinjar, District Banda, U.P.

SITE PLAN SHOWING NILKANTH TEMPLE, KALINJAR FORT

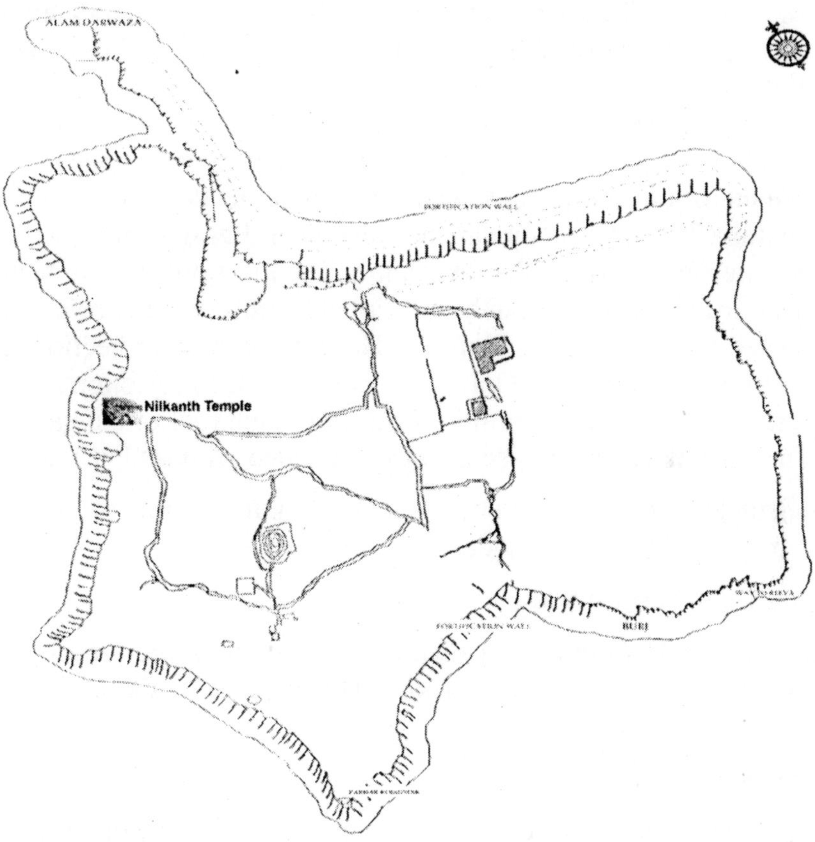

Fig. 14.2. Site plan showing location of Neelkanth temple, Kalinjar fort

and thickness at the base of the pillar is 2.45 m. and 0.60 m. respectively. There is an inscription at the base portion of the pillar.

The facade (Pl. 6) of the cave has been very rich, but it is now much broken and hidden by numerous coats of white wash.[1] Several layers of lime and ochre are clearly visible on the facade. The facade is adorned with four big lotus medallions in four separate frames. The sockets on the lotus and frame are an indication of some kind of attachment fixed over them. This seems to be a later addition. This portion covers half portion of the main opening. Both the side walls of the entrance passage possess inscriptions and rough sketches (Pl. 7) of the human figures. The maximum width of the entrance-passage is 2.28 m. Above the lotus medallions in the centre a miniature figure of lord Ganesha shown sitting with his devotees. On the top, the human sculptures in sitting posture are not very clear. Besides, the figures of Ganga and Yamuna are carved out on the door jamb. The most noteworthy feature of the temple is its projections (Fig.3) on the exterior side walls of the *garbha-griha*. They are ornamented with beautiful sculptures. The plan of these projections looks like the plan of Orissan temple style. Only lower portion of the projection is occupied by the sculptures. The total height of this portion from the roof of the garbha griha is 7.60 m. The mouldings at the base are also decorated with sculptured panels.

Interestingly, both the sides possess similar figures. Some of the outstanding sculptures may be described as under:

1. Standing Uma-Maheshwara :

Standing *Uma-Maheshwara* depicted underneath lotus arch. Face of Uma and right leg, ears and right hand of Siva lost. This belongs to the Chandella period (Pl.8).

2. Standing Nandi :

Four armed *Nandi* has been depicted in personified form, standing under Makara-torana. At the left side another *Nandi* is shown in miniature form (Pl. 9).

3. Scene of Musicians :

Right side panel depicts a female dancer with a male drummer. Both the persons are surrounded by a male dancer on either side. In the left side panel a female dancer is shown between a drummer and a flute player on either side (Pl. 10)

4. Goddess Yamuna :

A standing figure of *Yamuna* in beneath lotus creeper painted in red, badly damaged. It belongs to Chandella period (Pl. 11).

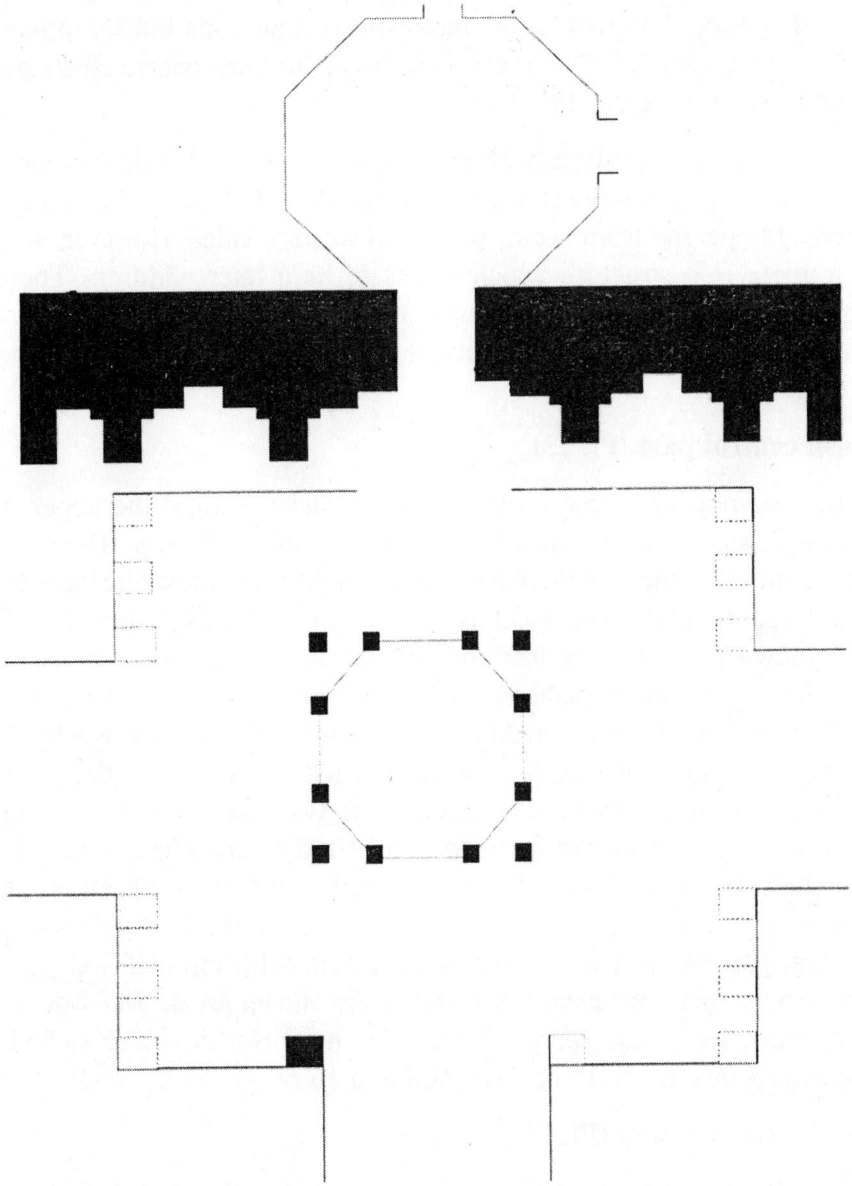

Fig. 14.3. Plan of Neelkanth temple, Kalinjar fort (not to scale)

There is a 1.45 m. wide open passage between *garbha-griha* and the *mandapa*. The *mandapa* (Fig. 3) consists of 12 ornamental pillars, four at the centre and four on the either side. The roof of the *mandapa* is now gone but the pillars and the pilasters form a square. The corners were cut off to form octagonal shapes that the roof looks like an octagon (Pl.12).

The *mandapa* is slightly elevated from the passage. Floor of the *mandapa* was damaged and it was re-set recently by the A. S I. Plan of the *mandapa* is tri-ratha with an opening from north, south and western sides. However, at the southern side there is a structure which seems to be a later addition. There are the evidences of the pillars along the openings. The pillars are huge and decorated with floral designs and sculptures. The central four pillars of both inner and outer sides are of same pattern.

Pillars in central part (Pl. 13)

The base portion of the pillars is square and two tired the upper one being smaller, which is decorated with *chaitya* arch motif on the top. The arch window motifs are shown in the middle of the various moldings. Above the base the pillar is decorated with floral designs which finish with in an arched design. This portion of pillar is shown with three projections the central one being wider. These projections further meet with an octagonal shaft decorated with floral design. Above the octagonal shaft another octagonal band decorated with floral design has been provided. Above the octagonal band a fluted shaft with same kind of design at the base is provided carefully. Above the fluted shaft two load bearers are depicted in brackets which are supported by wide floral band in circular manner. Above this circular shaft, two load bearing figures, the pillar capital have been provided. The circular shaft is crowned with fine finish circular tires diminishing in size. The upper most part of the circular tire is decorated with circular and diamond cut designs. Above this, four armed *Keechakas* are shown an all four sides. They are adorned with jewelry and sacred thread. The height of the pillar is 8.90 m. The mandapa measures are 11.15 m. east-west and 15.60 m. north- south.

Pillars of outer corners (Pl. 14) :

The pillar has three projections and decorated with floral design at the shaft but at the base portion is same as described in the case of pillars of inner side. There is a square band at the middle. The capital of the pillar is consisting of several decorated moldings increasing in sizes.

In addition, there was a row of six pillars in northern and southern sides along the opening of the *mandapa*. However, two pillars were erected in the front of the mandapa but one pillar which is vertically half chopped off right now available. Flat beams of octagon roof, are also decorated in two separate bands the lower one bears diamond cut palate with sun motif in between miniature pilasters while the upper band is shown with floral design. The floor of the *mandapa* is octagon in shape and having a hawan-kunda at the centre. Platform measures 5.95 m. from both north-south and east west. Mouldings around the mandapa are decorated with panels of floral designs and miniature *chaitya* window motifs.

So far as the date of the temple is concerned the gradual addition and development in the temple is seen. The *garbha-griha* seems to have been excavated prior to Chandella period as the sculptures on the pillars on *dwarssakhas* are suggesting. The sculptures on the exterior wall of the *garbha-griha* and pillared mandapa are of Chandella period. However, the floral designs which finish with in an arched design seem to be the impact of Muslim architectural style. Most probably an effort was made to preserve this temple during Islamic period too. The sculptures of *Ganga-Yamuna* on the door-jab are supposed to be of Gupta or late Gupta periods. Cunningham placed them in Gupta time bracket. If we look into the development of cave temple in India, Neelkanth temple was an advancement of this kind of style which was started at Udaigiri, (M.P.) in 6th *c.* A.D.

Acknowledgement:

I pay my deep gratitude to Shri I.D. Dwivedi, Superintending Archeologist of the Lucknow Circle who has permitted me to deal with the architectural edifices of Kalinjar fort. I am also thankful to Mrs. Meeta Srivastava, Library and Information Assistant for her valuable help in finding the related texts.

References

1. *District Gazetteers of Banda*, pp. 287-288
2. Cunningham, A., *Report of a tour in Bundelkhand and Rewa* in 1883-84.
3. *The Forts of India*.
4. *Ajaygarh Aur Kalinjar Ki Dev Pratimayen*.

15

DISCOVERY OF REMAINS OF ASOKAN PILLAR AT KACHHI GHAT—PATNA CITY

—*Capt. Pran Ranjan Prasad**

INTRODUCTION

The ancient city of Pataliputra occupies an honoured place in the history of India in general and 'Madhya Desa' or Magadh in particular. Being city of Seat of Power of the Imperial Mauryans, not only it basked in the glory for certuries, but also became a mute witness to the rise and fall of many dynasties to follow.

The Mauryan Pesiod was characterised by vigorous activities in the field of art and architecture under active and direct encouragement and initiatives of the kings, especially the Emperor Asoka. The empaeror's conversion to Buddhism after Kalinga war has been considered a turning point in the history of India and promotion of Buddhism. Asoka erected Pillars and issued a series of edicts and got them inscribed on these Pillars to ensure that the religion is followed as per established traditions and the unity of Buddhist Sangha is strengthened

Dr. Vasudev Sharan Agrawal[1] rightly says :

"The cream of Asokan Art consists of its monolithic stone pillars with imposing capitals, which speak not only the artistic excellence combined with technical skill but also much originality of thought on the part of the Emperor under the two fold scheme as explained above of marking of sacred spots of Buddhism and its centres and boundary of Madhya Desa". Asoka erected many pillars.

---

* Officer on Special Duty, Union Public Service Commission, New Delhi

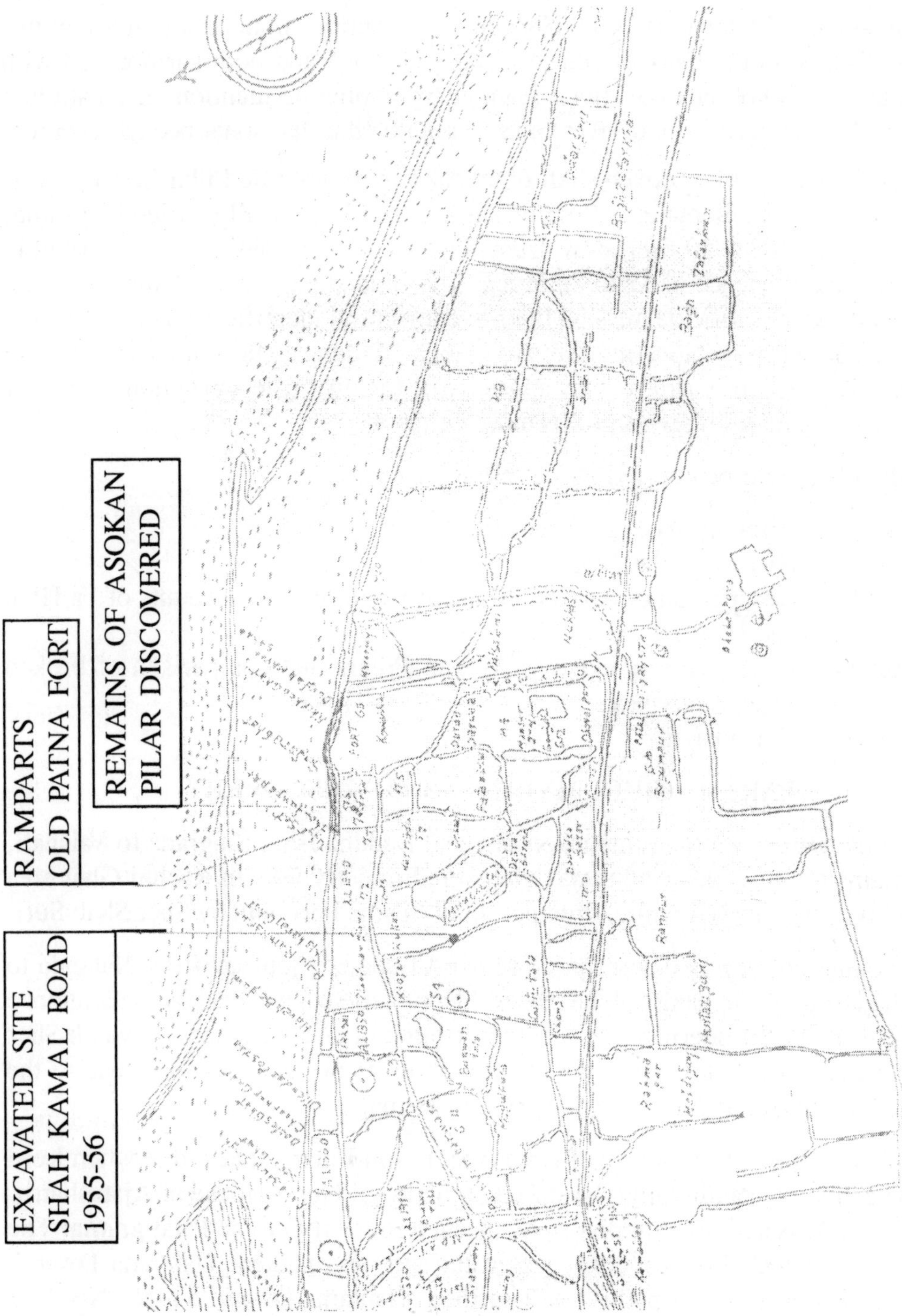

Fig. 15.1. Old bed of River Sone

The accounts of Chinese Scholars Fa Hsien and Hieun Tsang, who visited India in 4th and 7th Century A.D. respectively, mention about the existence of two Asokan Pillars on the bank of Ganges, both inscribed and both surmounted with Lion Capital. Oot of the two, Hieun Tsang is too explicit to mention the location of Pillar on the Southern Bank of river Ganges[2] but no pillar has so far been discovered.

The discovery of a broken shaft of an Asokan monolithic Pillar in early 90's, which has a susface diameter of 26.5 inches and stands vertically buried in ground, approximately 40 to 50 feet away from the ramparts of old Patna Fort (within Precinct); and presence of Mauryan bricks and sand stone lintels of varying sizes, may now definitely provide missing links in conjectural identification of the ancient city of Pataliputra and locating the two Asokan Pillars as described by Chinese scholars. Though, the narrative may appear to be too inrtricate and tedious, however it will be interesting on accourt of its ultimate result.

The paper will be covered in the following parts:

Part I. Circumstances of Discovery.
Part II. History of the Area.
Part III. Description of Asokan Pillars at Pataliputra in accounts of Fa Hien and Hieun Tsang.
Part IV. Description of existing Asokan Pillars and comparison of broken Monolithic shaft.
Part V. Conclusion.

PART I. CIRCUMSTANCES OF DISCOVERY

While tracing out the route taken by Losd Buddha from Rajgraha to Vaishali, the remains of an Asokan Pillar was discovered in early 90's in Kachhi Ghat area Patna City, which is well within Precincts of old Patna Fort built by Sher Shah Suri.

Literary sources give description of Lord Buddha's journey from Nalanda to Vaishali giving ancient names of the places. Identification of ancient places mentioned in these texts with modern names, and description of circumstances in which Sher Shah Suri decided to construct the Patna Fort in its present location close to the historic Gurudwara at Patna City is very interesting.

Dr. S. R Roy[3] in "Itinerary of Lord Buddhas in Bihar" states, that when Lord Buddha asrived at Pataligrama, he stayed at the Royal Guest House of Ajatashatru. At this time Vassakar and Sunitha were engaged in fortifying the Pataligrama. The gate through which Lord Buddha passed the city was named 'Gautama Dwara'. The noted historian H. Tripathi[4] has identified 'Gautama Dwara' a place North of Patna City Gurudwara. (The birthplace of Guru Govind Singhji).

The road North of Gurudwara bifurcates after approximately 100 to 150 yards, one goes towards the west on the southern Bank of Ganges and the other to the east of mosque known as Madarsa Mosque. Most of the area is inhibited but there exists an cpen courtyard immediately east of the mosque. The mosque is situated in the extreme western part of the old Patna Fort well within the precinct. One gets a very good view of the Ganges from the partially damaged old rampart on the northern end of the open courtyard of Patna Fort. A large round stone piece protruding 3 inches to 4 inches above the ground in the open space can vary well be noticed. The exposed portion suggested that the stone piece lied buried On close scrutiny, it became clear that it was part of a long stone column and the upper surface had been chiselled to make it plain. The exposed portion of the stone had some shine, which is akin to ether sandstone columns found at other places.

The location of this stone piece in open ground was barely 50 feet away from the southern Bank of river. About 5 to 6 feet away frem this stone piece was a water tank with large bricks and long sand stone lintels at the base. More number of similar lintels could be found while walking up the rampart. Some semicircular sandstone pieces were noticed embedded on the steps going down the river. Some eldesly people of the area confirmed that about 30 to 40 years back the stone shaft was protruding 3 to 4 feet above the ground, but now only this much portion was visible due to filling of earth raising the ground level.

PART II. HISTORY OF THE AREA

It is not just the location of buried broken monolithic Chunar sandstone shaft, but also the history of the area of discovery, which points out to the possibility of existence of an Asokan Pillar in the very area. This will be dealt briefly as per three separate periods of History', since this has a direct bearing on the discovery and arriving at the conclusion.

Pataligrama 5th Century B.C.:—River trade has been knoun to exist since early Vedic period through the great river Ganges. Control of trade through the river was one of the main issues of war between Magadh King Ajatasatru and Vajjis of Vaishali. Buddhist and Jain sources inform us that the war between the two kingdorm arose over dispute of control of river port at Ganges. Vajjis controlled the northern half while the southern half was under the control of the Magadh King, However, Vajjis used to make repeated incursions in the southern half and used to oust the people of 'Pataligrama' for months together affecting the revenue and trade of Magadh Empire. It was this reason coupled with his resolve to destroy mighty Lichhavis, the Magadh King decided to fortify the strategic village of Pataligrama.

It was during the time of fortification of 'Pataligrama' that Lord Buddha had stayed at the Royal Guest house of Ajatasatru at 'Pataligrama' enroute Nalanda to Vaishali.

Period 4th to 7th Century:—During this pesiod, there are no direct evidences available which has any relationship with the history of the area. However, references made regarding existence of inscribed Asokan Pillars with Lion Capital, monasteries and stupa on the bank of Ganges near the old village of the City in the area Ni Li are available.

7th-16th Century:—It is a well-known fact that after decline of Imperial Guptas, the city of Pataliputra lost much of its importance and could not regain the past glay. Even Hieun Tsang has mentioned that it had become deserted. Further, during the region of Gaud and Karna Suvarna the city sufftred most. Though, Palas, especially Dharam Pala tried to redeem its glory but could not regain the status of Seat of Power.

From the time Bakhtiar Khilji made his first invasion, the capital shifted to Biharsharif and Pataliputra further: got relegated in the background till Sher Shah Suri shifted his own capital to rechristianed 'Patna'. As per Tarik-I-Daudi written by Pathan Chronicler Abdullah[5] and references in Tarik-i-Shershahi and Shershah and his times, Sher Shah, after his conquest of Punjab and Bengal had come to Patna. Worried by threat of invasions by his adversaries from Hajipur and Purnea he had decided to explore the Southern bank of Ganges. It was during this reconnaissance that he came across the heap of ruins of ancient fortifications. He became so much awestruck by the strategic and tactical location of the place that he decided then and there to build a fort. Thus the famous fort. of Mughal and British period was built in record time of two years *i.e.* 1540-41.

Dr. Qeyammudin[6] rightly says:

"It seems that after halcyon days as the imperial Capital of Mauryas and Guptas, Pataliputra got relegated to the position of a small town.........and construction of fort at Patna by Sher Shah and its selection as the capital naturally once again recived its fortune and importance".

The aim is to highlight the similarity of the area of 'Patna Fort' with that of the ancient fortifications at 'Pataligrama' of Ajatasatru. The presence of Mauryan bricks and sand stone lintels extensively used in the ramparts of the fort which is now in poor condition, are its ample proof.

PART III. ASOKAN PILLARS IN ACCOUNTS OF FA-HSIEN AND HIEUN TSANG

The noted Chinese scholars Fa Hsien and Hieun Tsang visited ancient Pataliputra in 4th and 7th century A.D. respectively. Fa Hsien had noticed only six Asokan Pillars while, Hieun Tsang mertioned fifteen pillars. The difference in number can be basically attributed to the different routes taken by them and the duration of their stay.

(a) **Fa Hsien[7]:**—He has mentioned about the existence of two Asokan Pillars, both inscribed and surmounted by Lion Capital at Pataliputra There was a Vihara having Lord Buddha's footprints and an Asokan Stupa near one of the pillars. Another pillar was about three to four hundred paces to the north of stupa in the city NI-LI. This pillar had inscriptions, which mentioned the year and the circumstances of foundation of the city.

(b) **Hieun Tsang's Description of Asokan pilars at Pataliputra:**—This is more explicit. Some relevant paragraphs are quoted here from Sameul Beal's "The life of Hieun Tsang":

"....To the south of the river there is an old town about seventy Li in circuit. Although, it is waste and desolate, the parapets of wall still remain. To the north of the old palace, (precinct) boradering on the river Ganges, is a little town; this town has about 1000 houses; the north of the Palace there is a stone pillar several tens of feet high, this is the pillar whetre Asoka made the hell (place of torture).......To the south of the place of torture is a Stupa, this is one of the 84000 which the King built by aid of human artificers. Within it is a measure of relics of Tathagata .... Again there is a Vihara in which is a stone on which Tathagata walked: on the Stone is an impression of feet of Buddha in length a foat. and nine inches and in breadth six inches. .... To the north of Vihara is a stone column about thirty feet high; on this pillrar' is written a record that Asokaraja three times gave the whole of Jambudwipa in charity to Buddha, Dhawra, Samgha and three times bought back his inheritance (his Empire) with Jewels and Treasure".

PART IV. COMPARISON OF DISCOVERED MONOLITHIC SHAFT WITH THE EXISTING ASOKAN PILLARS

Though, Emperor Asoka erected a large number of pillars in different parts of his kingdom, evidences are not available to suggest the exact number of such pillars. The detail of existing Asokan pillars till day is attached as appendix.

Gen,. Cunningham[8] who had carried out a detailed study of the characteristics of Asokan pillars had found a general pattern of their making and had come to the conclusion that tapering of all the Asokan pillars from base upwards was at an average of 0.39 inches per foot.

Details of discovered remnants (Shaft):

(a) Location : 45 to 50 feet South of ramparts of northern ramparts of old Patna Fort.

(b) Diameter : 26.5 inches (67.2 cm.)

(c) Relative height of surface level in relation to present level of Ganges : 30 to 35 feet

Taking into account, Gen. Cunningham's formulae of reduction of 0.39 inches per foot and taking the base diameter of Pillar at Lauria Nandangarh (*i.e.* 35.5 inches) for calculation purposes, the height of the buried portion under the ground should be around 18 to 19 feet. Another point, which should be considered in this regard, is that the excavations at Kumhrar and Shah Kamal Road at Patna City had revealed Mauryan level at a depth of 10 to 12 feet. The spot of the buried shaft is much higher and therefore the above conclusion is a positive indication of our assumptions.

PART V. CONCLUSION

If:—

(a) The description of Lord Buddha's Journey from Nalanda to Pataliputra as given in various Buddhist texts is true?

(b) The accounts of Fa Hsien and Hieun Tsang's description regarding existence of Asokan Pillars on the southern bank of the Ganges are true?

(c) The accounts given by various historians regarding the making of 'Patna Fort' on ancient ruins by Sher Shah are true?

(d) The identification of 'Gautama Dwara' of Buddhist texts with area north of present Gurudwara at Patna City is true?

(e) The existence of Mauryan bricks and sand stone lintels recycled and used in various structure be any indications?

Then:—

The antiquity of the area goes to Mauryan Period and the existence of an Asokan Pillar in such a sacred place, which Buddhist texts refer as 'Gautama

Dwara' can be beyond doubt. Detailed excavation and further study can only give confrmatiom in this regard.

REFERENCES

1. Dr. V. S. Agrawal, *Indian Art*, p. 93.
2 Shaman Hwul Li & Sannnual Beal, *Life of Hie un Tsang*, pp. 101-102
3. Dr. S. R. Roy, *The Itinerary of Buddha in Bihar*, Appx. II, Comprehensive History of Bihar.
4. H. Tripathi, *Buddha Dharma and Bihar.*
5. Shaik Abdur Rashid, *Tarik-i-Daudi-'Abdulla'*, Aligarh, 1969.
   K. R. Qanungo, *Sher Shah and his times.*
   Imamudin, *The Tarik-I-Shershahi.*
6. Dr. Qeyammnudin, *Bihar under Pathan Rule.*
7. J. Legge, *A record of Buddhist kingdom by Fa Hsien.*
8. Gen. Cunningham, *Corpus Inscription Indicarum*, Vol. I, pp. 32-42

DETAIL OF EXISTING ASOKAN PILLAR

***Refs.:* Corpus inscriptions indicarum Vol. I, Gen Cunningham**
Indian Art - Dr. V. S. Agarawal

S.N.	*Location*	*Length of Shaft*	*Diameter of Shaft*		*Inscription*	*Capital*	*Remarks*
			Base	*Top*			
1.	Kolhua	36'	50"	37"	-	Single Lion	Believed to be earliest
2.	Lauria Areraj	36' 5"	41.8"	36.7"	Inscribed	-	Edicts in north 18" lines South 23 lines
3.	Lauria Nandangarh	32' 9.5"	35.5"	26.2"	Inscribed	Lion Capital	Capital 6'10" Bell shaped
4.	Sarnath	15.25 M	27.99"	21.75"	Inscribed	Four Lions seated back to back	Now only 2.03 M of broken shaft in situ
5.	Allahabad	35'	35"	26"	Queen's edict	-	Brough to Allahabad by Akbar
6.	Ram Purya (Two Pillars)	Both burried in water, Edicts similar to ser				2 & 3, damaged	Bull and Lion Capitals Found
7.	Sanchi	-	-	-	Inscribed	Four lions seated back to back	Only lower part of shaft in situ
8.	Delhi (a) Ex Topra	43' 7"	38.8"	25.3"	All seven edicts inscribed		(a) also known as golden pillar
	(b) Ex Meerut	Details not known					(b) Both pillars removed from original places by Feroz Tuglak
9.	Rummindei						
10.	Nilgiva						
11.	Bakror	(a) Details not available as either capital or shaft have been found					
12.	Taxila	(b) Locations based on accounts of Chinese travellers and other sources					
13.	Lathia	(c) List is not Exhaustive					
14.	Sankisa						
15.	Arra/Masarh						

Plate 1.I Red Polished ware from Satvahana Levels

Plate 1.II A view of residential complex of different Periods

Plate 1.III Stupa Mound before excavation

Plate 1.IV Stupa Mound during excavation

Plate 1.V Stupa after excavation and conservation - view from east

Plate 1.VI View of Stupa from south-west with later enlargement

Plate 1.VII The word (hla) inscribed on one of the steps of the enlarged platform

Plate 1.VIII Terracotta model of the stupa recovered from the excavation at Sirpur

Plate 2.I   Sirpur Copper plate

Plate 2.II   Sirpur Copper plate (Obverse)

Plate 2.III Sirpur Copper plate (Reverse)

Plate 2.IV Sirpur Copper plate

Plate 2.V   Sirpur Copper Mudra

Plate 2.VI   Sirpur Copper plate

Plate 2.VII Sirpur Copper plate (Obverse)

Plate 2.VIII Sirpur Copper plate (Reverse)

Plate 2.IX Sirpur Copper plate

Plate 2.X Sirpur Copper Mudra

Plate 2.XI Sirpur Copper plate

Plate 2.XII Sirpur Copper plate (Obverse)

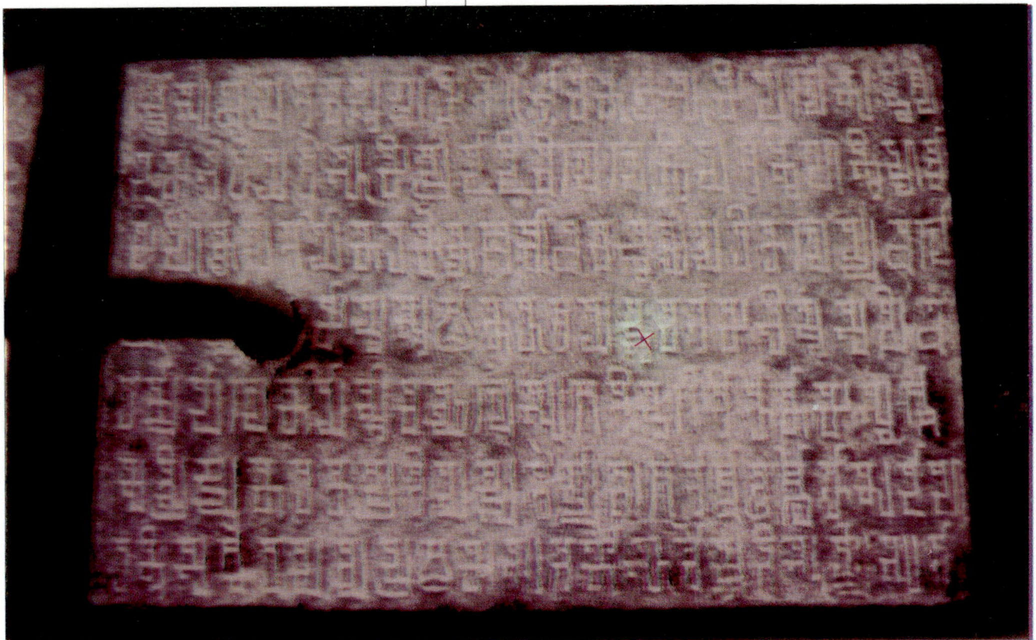

Plate 2.XIII Sirpur Copper plate (Reverse)

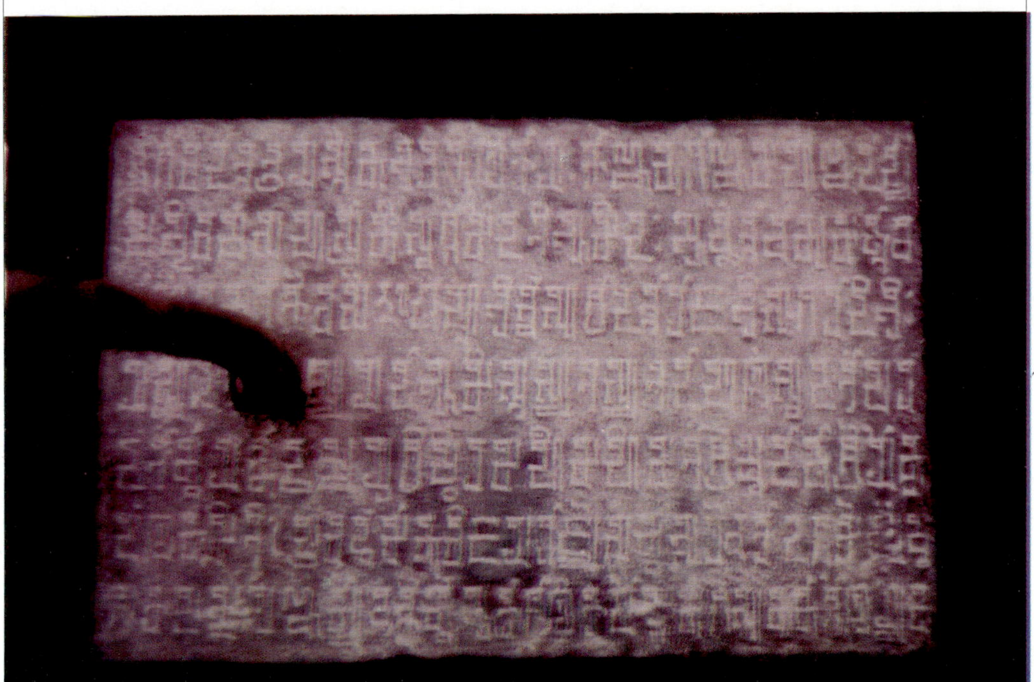

Plate 2.XIV Sirpur Copper plate

Plate 2.XV Sirpur Copper plate

Plate 2.XVI Sirpur Copper plate (Obverse)

Plate 2.XVII Sirpur Copper plate (Reverse)

Plate 2.XVIII Sirpur Copper plate

Plate 4.I Iron slag from leelar under electron microscope

Plate 4.II Iron slag from leelar under electron microscope

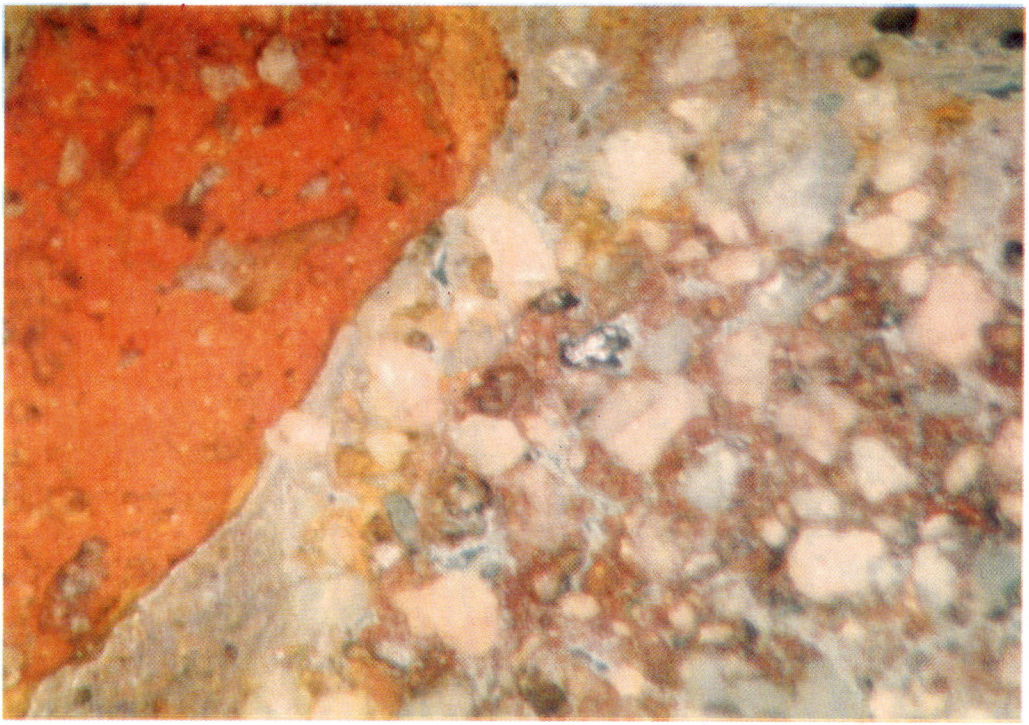

Plate 4.III Iron slag from leelar under electron microscope

Plate 5.I Black and red Ware

Plate 5.II Black Ware

Plate 5.III Micaceous red Ware

Plate 5.IV Painted Micaceous red Ware

Plate 5.V Micaceous red Ware

Plate 5.VI Lid of black Ware

Plate 5.VII Shells fragment

Plate 5.VIII Bone Point & chalcedony blade

Plate 5.IX Red slipped Ware, Historical Period

Plate 5.X Terracotta tile

Plate 5.XI Red slipped Ware, Historical Period

Plate 5.XII   Red Polished Ware

Plate 5.XIII   Pestles (Broken)

Plate 6.I   Revanta from Harnaul, Late Gupta, c.600 A.D.

Plate 6.II Revanta Image at Aring, Mathura, Pratihāra Period

Plate 6.III Revanta Image from Mandoi, Mathura, 9th century A.D.

Plate 8.I Sirpur SRP-32, View of Buddha Vihara from West

Plate 8.II Sirpur SRP-33, View of Trideva Temple Complex facing West

Plate 8.III Sirpur SRP-30, Parsvanath

Plate 8.IV Sirpur SRP-32 Buddha in Bhumisparsh Mudra

Plate 8.V Sirpur View of Street with row of houses on both sides

Plate 8.VI Sirpur a house complex with 10 rooms

Plate 8.VII Model of Stupa and Vajra

Plate 8.VIII Sirpur Buddha in Bhumisparsa Mudra

Plate 8.IX Sirpur Avalokitesvara Padmapani

Plate 8.X Sirpur Boddhisattva Samantabhadra

Plate 8.XI Sirpur Jambhala

Plate 8.XII Sirpur Tara

Plate 8.XIII Sirpur Prajnaparamita

Plate 8.XIV Shahjahan's Silver coin (Obverse)

Plate 8.XV Regnal Year 6, Patna Mint (Reverse)

Plate 8.XVI Shahjahan's Silver coin (Obverse)

Plate 8.XVII Regnal Year 33, Surat Mint (Reverse)

Plate 8.XVIII Aurangzeb's Silver coin (Obverse)

Plate 8.XIX Mint Bander-e-Mubarak, Surat (Reverse)

Plate 8.XX Aurangzeb's Silver coin (Obverse)

Plate 8.XXI Regnal Year 12, Surat Mint (Reverse)

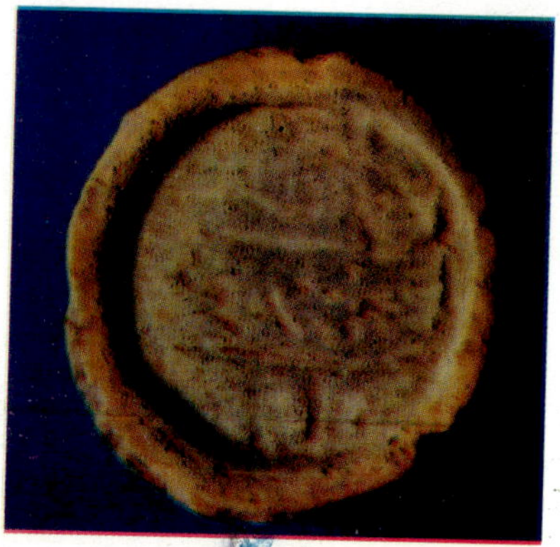

Plate 8.XXII T.C. Seal with Persian Legends Mughal Periods Impression of Aurangzeb's Silver coin

Plate 9.I Jamuanua - Mound I

Plate 9.II Jamuanua - Uma Maheshwar

Plate 9.III Jamuanua - Mahisasuramardini

Plate 9.IV Kamhari Dih-Pottery

Plate 9.V Rampur-Pottery

Plate 9.VI Manihari - Pottery

Plate 10.I Badhi Mound, Choudwar, Dist: Cuttack, Orissa
(Before Excavation)

Plate 10.II Structures (Temple remains) of Phase I and II,
Excavated Badhi mound, Choudwar, Dist: Cuttack, Orissa

Plate 10.III Entrance stone (Chandrasila) of Phase-I found in Phase-II, Excavated Badhi mound, Choudwar, Dist.: Cuttack, Orissa (close up view)

Plate 10.IV Retaining wall of Mud rampart, Bharandi, Choudwar, Dist.: Cuttack, Orissa

Plate 10.V Mutilated Jain sculpture, near Bharandi, Choudwar, Dist.: Cuttack, Orissa

Plate 10.VI Architectural fragments, Tokeijhada, Choudwar, Dist.: Cuttack, Orissa

Plate 10.VII Kedareswar Mahadeva Temple, Choudwar, Dist.: Cuttack, Orissa.

Plate 10.VIII Mandiracharini Kedareswar Mahadeva Temple complex, Choudwar, Dist.: Cuttack, Orissa.

Plate 10.IX Lion, Kedareswar Mahadeva Temple complex, Choudwar, Dist.: Cuttack, Orissa.

Plate 10.X Uttareswar Mahadeva Temple, Choudwar, Dist.: Cuttack, Orissa.
(Before conservation)

Plate 10.XI Mutilated sculpture pieces, Badieswa temple complex, Choudwar, Dist.: Cuttack, Orissa.

Plate 10.XII Pieces of decorative entrance frame, Narabudi, Choudwar, Dist.: Cuttack, Orissa

Plate 10.XIII Rock-cut caves, Indrani pahara, Choudwar, Dist.: Cuttack, Orissa

Plate 11.I Cup marks

Plate 11.II Historical scene on the rock at Kujota

Plate 11.III Historical scene on the rock at Kujota

Plate 11.IV Cup marks

Plate 14.I Neelkanth Temple, a general view, Kalinjar fort, (view from north)

Plate 14.II Door opening at the right of lingam, Neelkanth Temple, Kalinjar fort

Plate 14.III Facade of the cave, Neelkanth Temple (view from west)

Plate 14.IV Inscription and rough sketches of human figures, Neelkanth Temple (view from south-west)

late 14.V a Uma-Maheshwar, Neelkanth Temple

Plate 14.V b Standing Nandi, Neelkanth Temple

Plate 14.VI Dancing human figure on the panels, exterior of Neelkanth Temple, Kalinjar fort

Plate 14.VII Human devotees on wall panel, garbha-griha Neelkanth Temple (view from south-east)

Plate 14.VIII a   Pillar of Inner side

Plate 14.VIII b   Pillar of outer corners